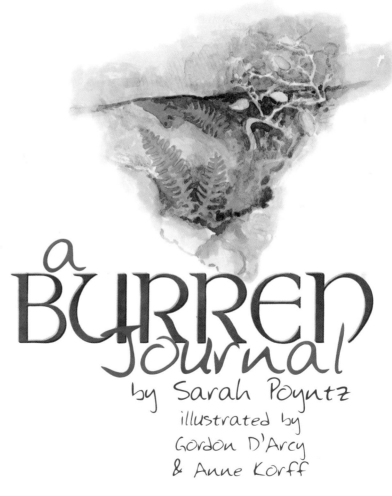

a BURREN
Journal

by Sarah Poyntz

illustrated by
Gordon D'Arcy
& Anne Korff

Text first published by The Guardian ©.

This collection published in 2000 by Tír Eolas ©,
Newtownlynch, Kinvara, Co. Galway.

Written by Sarah Poyntz.
Selected and edited by Alan Smart.
Illustrated by Gordon D'Arcy © and Anne Korff ©.
Photographs on page 14 the Burns family; page 16
Beth O'Connell; page 20 Michael Irwin and Eithne
O'Reilly; page 41 The Examiner; page 49 painting
Manus Walsh ©.

ISBN 1 873821 13 1

British Library Cataloguing in Publication Data.
A catalogue record for this book is available from
the British Library.

Cover and layout: Anne Korff and Johan Hofsteenge
Typesetting: Johan Hofsteenge
Printed in Ireland by Betaprint

Dedication

I dedicate this book to my friend Mary Ann Radzinowicz, her children Annie and William, my late family and to my cousins in Ireland and in New Zealand.

Acknowledgements

It gives me great pleasure to thank the *Guardian* newspaper for choosing me to fill a vacancy in the *Country Diary* column. I owe a great deal to my first editors, Chris McLean and Jeannette Page, for their helpfulness, encouragement and loyalty. I thank their successors and add my tribute to a great newspaper for its humane decency. My gratitude extends to the readers of the *Country Diary*, many of whom write to me and some of whom visit me. They are my friends.

I also wish to thank my publisher, Anne Korff of Tír Eolas, and my editor for this collection, Alan Smart. Not just for undertaking this project but for doing so with such professional expertise, zest, and friendliness.

Anne Korff and Gordon D'Arcy have embellished the book with their watercolours and drawings. I have no doubt that the book will be mainly bought and treasured for their beautiful work. How could I ever repay them? My friend, the artist Manus Walsh, kindly gave permission to use his painting *Burren Moon Rising*, which I am glad to say we own, in the book.

My friend Mary Ann Radzinowicz, to whom this book is dedicated, was an unfailing help throughout the project. Indeed, it was she, together with my friend, Nora O'Connor (nee French) of Waterford, my friends, Rita Guerlac and her daughter Lucy, of Ithaca, New York State, Liane Elledge and her late husband, Professor Scott Elledge, who encouraged me to seek out Anne Korff in order to have these diaries published. I acknowledge my debt to my friends and past students for their encouragement. Friends in Ireland, especially my childhood friends Nora O'Connor (nee French) and Kitty Heslin (nee Conran), my friend Peggie Quigley and her late husband, Matt, Bridie and Seán Byrne, all of New Ross, Co. Wexford. My friends in Ithaca, New York State, Professors Mary C. Rossiter, Sandra Siegel, Jean Blackall, Beth Teskey, Gordon Teskey and the members of the Ithaca Drama Club. Elsewhere in the United States, Professors Anne Shaver, Susanne Woods, Julia Walker, Joe Wittreich and Stuart Curran. My French friends, Marie France and Philippe Lacaze of the Medoc and Colette and Pierre Etienne Guerin of Burgundy. My Cornish friends especially Marie Martin and her daughters; my friends in Cambridge, in particular Jane Bednarczyk, the late Karen Leighton, Kate Teicher, Judith Chisholm, Judith Braid, Alison Duke and the late Professor Muriel C. Bradbrook and my friend, Margie Kirk of Stratford on Avon.

I thank the dear people of Ballyvaughan and the local area for their kindness, paying my respectful tribute to McNeill O'Loghlen. His helpful friendship, together with that of his late wife May, was invaluable to us in settling into village life. His unique knowledge, his stories and his directions to places of interest in the Burren enabled me to write many of the diaries in this book. I salute you McNeill, our Prince of the Burren.

We have been blessed with excellent close neighbours since 1986: Mick Carrucan, Brenda and Padraic Cleary, the Burns, Irwins, Doolins, Linnanes, Martins, Monks and O'Donoghues. Maura Mooney-Hynes has helped us greatly since we came to the village. In addition I thank George and Mary Keegan, and their children and their spouses. Our dear friends, as well as our weekly luncheon companions, Beth O'Connell, Bernadette Monks, Mary Keegan and Bonnie Wicks have all given Mary Ann and myself many a laugh. Tom O'Halloran, Mary Ellen and their children have never let us down. I thank the Burren Action Group for their nine-year struggle to save our beautiful Mullaghmore from destruction.

Lastly, I am indebted to my family. My late parents, Nellie Poyntz (nee Murphy) of Wexford town and my father, Frank Poyntz, solicitor of New Ross Co. Wexford, who gave me the gift of life. My late siblings Kitty and Jack and my late aunts, Alice and Maimie. My cousins here in Ireland: Aine and Jack Kenny, Campile, Co. Wexford, Aileen and Piers O'Hallahan, Rathloose, Clonmel, Co. Tipperary, Mary and Tim O'Driscoll, Glanmire, Co. Cork, Anna Curtin, Rosslare, Co. Wexford, Emma and Michael Broaders, Dundalk, Co. Louth, Eddie Poyntz and his wife, New Ross, Co. Wexford. My Poyntz cousins in Omagh: Claire (Linnane), Frank Poyntz and his wife and their son Gerard and his wife, Teresa, who was injured in the Omagh bombing. In New Zealand my Murphy cousins, Joan, Pat and Maire and in Indonesia Professor Murt Murphy.

Foreword

Sarah Poyntz's diaries are a superb example of the very special relationship that the Burren evokes in so many people who were fortunate to be born there, to live and work there or who return, time and time again, to visit this unique landscape. The hallmarks of this special relationship are love, understanding, respect and, above all, delight - all of which are richly demonstrated in the selection of diaries in *A Burren Journal*.

Sarah writes, not only of the beauty and diversity of the flowers and ferns in the grykes and meadows, the shy pine marten and the Burren hare, but of the magnificence of the terraced mountains, the fissured, layered shoreline, the winding rural lanes with their species-rich hedges and verges. But, more importantly, the diaries capture the "lived in" sense of the Burren landscape and the evidence of a centuries-old, harmonious relationship between people and place. This is illustrated by the tombs and ruined churches, the remains of terraced gardens and once-peopled villages, the dry stone walls of ancient and more recent origin. The Irish placenames tell of long-forgotten relationships between the Burren and its people, and the traditional farming practices that have sustained a farming community and conserved a unique element of the Irish heritage. Even more importantly, the diaries illustrate the sense of place, the humour, the friendliness, the music, the culture that make the village and farming communities of the Burren unique in the true sense of landscape – i.e. people and place.

A Burren Journal is published at a time when a nine-year conflict over the siting of visitor facilities at Mullaghmore has come to an end. It also comes at a time when the pawmarks of the Celtic Tiger are having an increasingly negative imprint on the Burren land and seascapes. It comes at a difficult time for the farming community of the Burren and at a time of opportunity for those who wish to exploit the Burren for short-term, and environmentally-damaging financial gain.

It is my hope that these diaries of love, respect and appreciation will encourage all of us who love the Burren, whether as inhabitants or visitors, to work together for its sustainable development and conservation in the harmony that has characterised the relationship between people and place in the Burren over the centuries.

Emer Colleran

I was born in New Ross, Co. Wexford in 1926. My parents came from opposite sides in the politics of our country but as they were civilised and loved each other this did not impinge adversely on us their children – in fact it made life more interesting. My father, Frank Poyntz, was a solicitor. My mother was the daughter of Captain Larry Murphy who sailed tea clippers from Liverpool to China and India and other sailing ships to America and the Far East. We were brought up to value the important things in life, literature, art and music, and this was continued at my secondary education by the Loreto Order at Loreto Abbey in Gorey, Co. Wexford. My luck in this held when I went to University College, Dublin where my professor was Dr. Lorna Reynolds. I cannot express how much I owe Professor Reynolds, who I am proud to say is still my mentor and very dear friend.

My family was devastated when in 1936 my sister Kitty was drowned at the age of fifteen. I was ten and my brother was nineteen. The suffering of death and loss had to be faced, including the witnessing of the pain of my poor parents, their grief on the far side of words. The people of New Ross rallied supremely to our support and our relatives were superb.

In the 1950s I went, an exile, to earn my living as a teacher in London, then in Cornwall at Callington Grammar School and finally in Cambridge. I was awarded a fellowship to study for a term at Girton College, Cambridge in 1971. I had already been appointed head of the English department at the Perse School for Girls in Cambridge. At Girton I met my lifelong friend Professor Mary Ann Radzinowicz and her children Annie and William. Mary Ann was Director of Studies in English at Girton and a lecturer in the University of Cambridge. She is an American of Irish roots and I could talk to her in those terrible 1970s of the Troubles in Northern Ireland – about the needless death and devastation in these two islands.

After a few years at the Perse School I was asked to take up the position of Deputy Head, which I accepted. It was a position I never filled because of major surgery and consequent ill health. My friends in Cambridge were splendid and Mary Ann and her children were my unfailing support during these years of illness and recovery. On medical advice I took early retirement though I returned to the Perse School to teach part-time, helping students prepare for the Oxford and Cambridge Entrance Examinations in English. This was kindly arranged for me by the Headmistress, the late Miss Constance Bedson and my departmental colleagues, Kate Teicher and Judith Chisholm. I also taught some students in the Department of Classics of Girton College, preparing them for the Shakespeare paper in the Cambridge University final examinations. Ms Duke, Director of Studies in Classics at Girton, arranged this. Thanks to these friends I was able to survive financially.

I followed Mary Ann to America when she was appointed Professor of English at Cornell University in Ithaca, New York State, where she later held the Jacob Gould Schurman Chair of English Literature. We came to Ireland for holidays each year and were joined by Mary Anne's children. In 1983 we stayed in Ballyvaughan and we kept coming back until we finally settled here for our retirement – myself in 1986 and Mary Ann in the 1990s. Here we stay, our paradise regained, except for our annual holidays in France and occasional forays to the United States and Cornwall and other parts of England. Here I write, here I build my model ships, plank on frame and here I help Mary Ann in the garden, doing some of the rough work.

I have been contributing to the *Country Diary* column in the *Guardian* newspaper for over a decade, writing mainly about the Burren. My aim is to try to convey my love for, and joy and delight in, this most beautiful region, Ireland's greatest natural glory. I have scarcely touched on the threats to this most precious and fragile landscape. The threats are real and many, motivated by relentless greed and wilful invincible ignorance. And there are none so ignorant as those who do not want to know. The main perpetrators are the so-called developers, the builders of rabbit-hutch style houses, usually as holiday homes. There are now more holiday homes and second homes in this area than there are homes of year round residents. More of this type of 'development', if it can be described as such, or the building of yet more hotels and guest houses, is not advisable or sustainable. The only hope to prevent more of this kind of environmental destruction rests in the hands of the permanent residents of the Burren for politicians, whether local or national, cannot be allowed to ride roughshod over the will of the people. May wisdom and generosity of heart be paramount so that the Burren may be preserved for its children in this new century.

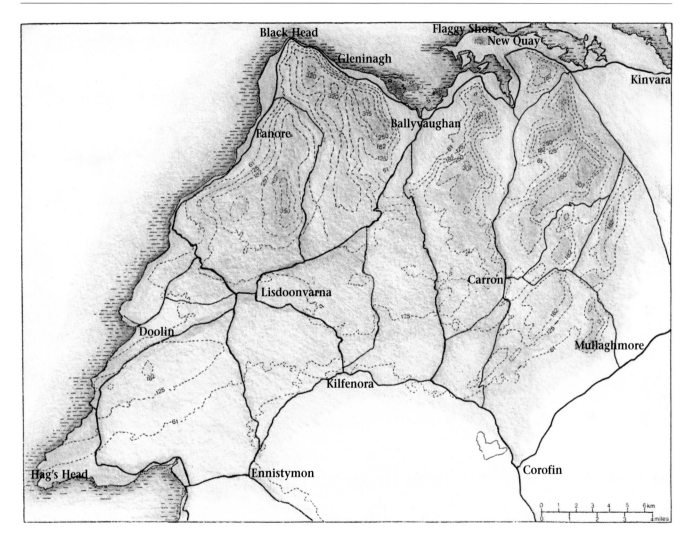

Guides and Maps of the Burren

J.W. O'Connell and A. Korff, *Ballyvaughan, Kilfenora* and *O'Brien Country*, illustrated rambler's guides and maps, Tír Eolas.

Tim Robinson, *The Burren*, Folding Landscapes.

Books on the Burren

G. Cunningham, *Burren Journey, Burren Journey North* and *Burren Journey West*.

G. D'Arcy and J. Hayward, *The Natural History of the Burren*, Immel, 1992.

J.W. O'Connell and A. Korff, *The Book of the Burren*, Tír Eolas, 1991.

E.C. Nelson and W.F. Walsh, *The Burren, a companion to the wild flowers of an Irish limestone wilderness*, 1997 (reprint).

E.C. Nelson, *Wild Plants of the Burren and the Aran Islands*, Collins Press, 1999.

A gryke with mosses and ferns.

March 1988

Here, on this coastal stretch of the Burren, wind is supreme, whether rip-roaring, insidious with promise or gentle in freshening hedges. The memory of 'the night of the Big Wind', long years since, still lingers. Indeed two years ago we experienced a mighty wind which turned the young, fresh leaves of thorn, hazel, ash and our own newly-planted fruit trees into a dull, curled black. Winter invaded our spirits at the sight of our spring blasted until people assured us all would be well. Within a few weeks nearly all the leaves straightened out and black gave way to green. So in one year we had two springs, never mind the two winters!

Now a storm shuddering in from the ocean has deposited just below the grass line on the Rine's small, silver beaches, huge mounds of sea tangle; tawny, nut-hazel, dark oak, amber, green-tinted with ribbons of rose weed commingled. Later it will be spread out, dried, sold to factories or used as fertiliser. Indeed on the nearby Aran Islands and throughout this West Coast it must have saved countless lives. For, mixed with rock pounded against rock by human hands, it made soil where there was little or none – the vintaged sea. Now clouds, great continents of them, are thrust helter-skelter across the grey sky, the rain coming in spates, then in light sprinkles, the wind crying with mighty blusters of sound, thinning off and on to

After the storm.

mere sighs. The storm has worn itself out. Peace is about to be reborn. The rockpool is quiet, a sea snail slowly inching its way forward. The sea raven (cormorant) has taken up its position on its favourite rock, the ringed plovers and oystercatchers trip lightly over the flats "with hey, ho the wind and the rain".

March 1991

Pigs, crinoids, rooks and "bother the flowers that bloom in the Spring", tra la! I watched, for at least six or seven minutes, a rook on a television aerial behind our house. Every so often it took several side steps, then became quite still until it raised its head, opened its strong, grey beak and emitted a repertoire of caws. After this recitative it took great, almost frustrated sideswipes at its highly untidy plumage. Then the whole pantomime was repeated. It went on so long and with such determined repetition that I was beginning to feel thwarted myself! Rescue arrived with the perching of another rook on the aerial. Immediately its cawing lover sidled up and both heads touched in silence. The relief! It reminded me of the infallible sign of spring in Ithaca, in upstate New York – the release of the Cornell University pigs

Limestone fossils.

into the open runs. Weeks before the crocuses might have bloomed only to be smothered and beaten to the ground by a few feet of snow but the sight of the hogs was sheer bliss. Recently we saw a farmer carrying a newborn lamb under each arm. Then we saw a most handsome bull, with the curliest red hair on his forehead and long, curled eyelashes and, leaning against his side, a beautiful heifer. He was gently licking her neck and her front legs were actually trembling. It is no wonder that the silken kine, the cow, became, in Gaelic poetry, a personification of Ireland, *a dhroimeann donn dílis* (beloved brown cow of the white back)! Later we loitered on the shore in front of Gleninagh Castle standing on and holding what was made and laid down over three hundred million years ago – limestone pavement underfoot and in fist, picked at random, a stone containing rings and rings of sea lilies (crinoids). Once their cup-shaped bodies and leathery arms waved and shifted and found sustenance beneath the moving waters, "here, millions of mixed shades and shadows, drowned dreams, somnambulisms, reveries; all that we call lives and souls, lie dreaming, dreaming still." (Melville).

March 1992

Wind, peace and dead counts. On a grey day, the wind whining and whipping, we climbed the fairly steep ascent to Oughtmama (the breast of the mountain pass) about five miles from Ballyvaughan, on the other side of the road from Corcomroe Abbey or St Mary of the Fertile Rock (c.1200 AD). We descended to the airy silence of the three ruined churches of Oughtmama. So sheltered is the site that, though higher up on Turlough Hill and its Iron Age ringfort the wind ripped and tore about, here all was calm. The churches, more ancient than Corcomroe Abbey, stand on older ecclesiastical sites probably pre-dating St Patrick's arrival – an older Christianity. We examined the water and baptismal fonts, the former with its two intertwined strange animals sculpted on the front. To the north of the churches lie the remains of terraced gardens, earthen constructions to channel water for the mill in a once

Holy water font and baptismal font at Ucht Máma church.

flourishing village. Here a man could stand, as today's farmer still can,

> "His rainy hills around him, the soft grass,
> Darkness of ragged hedges, and his earth
> The black, damp earth under the roots of trees."
> (Padraic Colum).

Sure enough the rain came to the hills and we were well drenched! Another day we explored part of the Doorus peninsula (*Dubh Ros:* thickly wooded promontory) on Galway Bay. The sea was quiet, shading from dark to pale translucent blue under a blue sky without a single cloud. In Parkmore graveyard we found the tomb of the Frenches and Counts de Basterot, the latter arriving in 1792, émigrés from the French Revolution. The most appealing of them was Florimond de Basterot whose name translates as Flora of the world (unite)! We watched brent geese feeding and further out great northern divers. At the end of February Welsh musicians paid their annual winter visit to Ballyvaughan to make music with their Irish contemporaries. The pubs were grand with voices and melody, as Shakespeare put it,

> "Orpheus with his lute made trees,
> And the mountain tops that freeze,
> Bow themselves when he did sing."

March 1995

"I do remember the house." Jimmy Burns' house was on the road to Black Head, its back looking out to the sea, neat, gleaming white. Its garden full of flowers and shrubs created and lovingly tended by his wife until her death, after that cared for by Jimmy out of loyalty and devotion to her lifelong caring. The opening sentence above was written to us by our friend Sandra Siegel, of Cornell University in the States. I quote it because many visitors and readers will remember the house and even more so Jimmy if they met him. He cared for things and for creatures though without sentimentality. He said to me once after his wife's death, "Ah! Sure I miss her all the time." Several times I saw him trot by on one of his horses – a

Jimmy Burns and his donkey Nellie and companion.

beautiful sight, the easefulness, the perfect synchronisation between man and animal. We were walking by his house one day when Jimmy emerged and asked, "Would you like to see the foal?" We said, "Yes." Jimmy whistled once – a short pause then mare and foal came trotting. We will never forget the pride of the man. He was a proud man and a witty one. On this occasion he asked, "How is the cat?" We told him she was fine and would soon be fifteen. Immediately a gleam of mischief came to his eyes. "Would you mind if I told Michael Monks that you're giving a birthday party for your cat?" "Not at all." The reported conversation: "They're giving a birthday party for the cat." "Are you going?" asked Michael. "Wouldn't miss it!" Michael duly recounted this to his wife, Bernadette, who told us. I asked her what Michael's reaction was, "He said, 'They're half-crackt.'" Yet the Monks' family (our good friends) had the vet come to the house when their sheepdog, Tulip, had to be put down and they were all with her to the end. Such people make a village. Our Jimmy died a few weeks ago. In his own words, "Ah! Sure we miss him all the time."

March 1996

The 25th February 1996, the day of peace demonstrations throughout Ireland, the dawn came slowly, pouring silver light across the sky, over the quiet waters of the bay. As the light strengthened multiple shades of grey spread everywhere, toning in with the Burren's grey stone walls, its hills with their patches of morning mist. The peace was tangible, "dropping from the veils of the morning" (Yeats), the peace of natural things. However the people of the village, population about 400, like the slightly over 98% of our Republic who oppose violence, were worried. Therefore, in the days of the week previous to the 25th February, a spontaneous desire to make a stand for peace, in opposing violence, grew until it was decided that we, like those in the big centres of population, would also march for peace in our own village on 25th February. So at 3 pm we gathered together with people from surrounding areas in the centre of Ballyvaughan – WE, THE PEOPLE, elderly, middle-aged, young, children with our home-made placards: GIVE BACK OUR PEACE -STOP KILLING. One little girl had designed her own poster: the Union Jack side by side with the Irish Tricolour, a hand from each flag reaching to clasp the other. With Father Kelly we marched, on a cold, glitteringly sunny day, standing for a minute's silence for the victims of terrorism (Canary Wharf and the Aldwych Bus bomb in all our minds). Then the Lord's Prayer was said and we dispersed. Yet again this marvellous village and region on Ireland's western coast manifested its worth, its mettle in the grand numbers taking part, in the openness of our demand for peace, our hands carrying nothing but paper posters. There was a lovely, easy unity among us when the intelligence to uphold our democracy was allied to the heart full of concern for the innocent dead and wounded both impelling us, minds and hearts beating as one, to walk for peace, "Still in thy right hand carry gentle peace." (Shakespeare).

March 1998

I could be paddling or swimming in warm tropical seas! However I was born some hundreds of millions of years too late. Difficult it is to believe that our Burren once lay under warm oceanic waters as I stand gazing at deposits of that time, the Burren's limestone pavements, the stone of its walls. Five thousand years ago Neolithic man built Newgrange in the east of our island – two hundred tonnes of stone transported over eighty kilometres. The drystone walls of the Burren and the Aran Islands may be more recent but they too are beautiful. There are 1,500 kilometres of them on the Aran Islands. There must be at least twice that in the Burren snaking as they do up and over and down the hills, across the fields, towards the sea, on the waters' edge, earth's fragile boundary. The walls are built on top of the rock from which time and weather split them. So no foundations are needed. Another advantage is that because of the gaps and holes in these walls the sheep won't jump them! Then there is the relationship of the walls to the landscape from which they seem to grow. The skill is in the positioning of each stone in relation to the others and in the sturdiness of the whole. They are not for climbing by human beings! Multi-shaped fissured stones are blocked together by long slabs, the roughness acting as traction to keep all in place. Sometimes there is a herringbone pattern and always there is the lichen, colour enriching with their greens, whites, startlingly vivid oranges fading to yellow (*Xanthoria*). A gap lined with this brilliant orange caught the light rays becoming gold, a miniature sun. Indeed colour, light and shade play upon and within the Burren's drystone walls enhancing its landscape with fine open-work, with tracery of stone and so, as Emerson says, "The conscious stone to beauty grew."

Drystone walls.

March 2000

Today we went to O'Loghlen's Pub in Ballyvaughan to buy our newspaper. Mary Ann handed McNeill O'Loghlen eighty-five pence in pennies and tuppences. McNeill looked at the fist-full of coins then at Mary Ann and said, "Been saving up, I see." He calls Mary Ann the Commander-in-Chief, recalling her father's position as a General in the United States Army, (he served with General Eisenhower in Strategic Planning in World War Two), and also hinting that she is boss in the house – not true.

Seán McNeill O'Loghlen 'Prince of the Burren'.

When we first came to Ballyvaughan to holiday in the rental cottages my brother Jack came to stay in his favourite Irish hotel, Hylands in Ballyvaughan. He went to O'Loghlen's, told McNeill he was my brother and McNeill said "Ah, the two ladies." We were delighted. Our McNeill is never lost for a quick comment, reply or witticism and our days have been made happier by them. He is a man of the old school whose word is his bond. He seems to be a grave and serious man, a man of reserve but we know that he is a man with a heart. He was driving me to Shannon Airport in 1986 and I told him the story of my sister's drowning. He said nothing, for there was nothing to be said except what would have been clichés, but I knew how touched he was. He does not wear his heart on his sleeve. He wears it in sympathy for the truly deserving and no chancer will fool McNeill. He will be seen for what he is. For years, in true neighbourliness, McNeill looked after our house in our absences, sometimes for six months at a time. We tried to put this on a business footing by offering him a fee, which he utterly scorned. During these absences McNeill would come to the house after the pub closed at night. He would switch on the lights and read books from our shelves, such as *Sir William Gregory of Coole* by Brian Jenkins. When McNeill's wife May became very ill and was about to return from hospital we thought this would be an opportunity to make some tangible return for all his kindness to us. So we gave May a remote control television which she could use from her bed, calculating that anything given to McNeill's May would also be a gift to himself. His gratitude was touching because he himself was so touched and he said "All my life I've been doing things for others and so often with no thanks at all." We respect and are fond of McNeill. He is, in truth, as his ancestors were before him, the Prince of the Burren.

April 1988

We are owners of our two and a half acres of Burren land for nearly three years. Even now we find it difficult to believe in our good fortune. We had been coming for years to the rental cottages in our village of Ballyvaughan, never dreaming we would live on land, backed by hills, looking out on Galway Bay. There were, of course, difficulties. The day our friend showed us this land we lost him, so deep and impenetrable were the thickets and thorn scrub. Our problem was to preserve the land as Burren while being able to walk it and view wildness a little tamed. We had scrub removed but preserved ash, hazel, holly and thorn trees. Between the drystone wall and the house front we had laid beautiful, local Moher, often called Liscannor, flagstones, leaving spaces for flowerbeds. I spent a hot day under the great claw of an earth shifter, signalling to the hero in the cab the exact location for huge boulders, a plan to give variety of height as well as acting as boundaries. At first we had a small Stonehenge! Everywhere we planted bulbs, heather, low bushes, all Burren plants being preserved. We kept discovering beauty after beauty, all previously smothered. In this ancient Celtic land so beloved by its poets and whose people so loved and respected them, we remember Shakespeare's words, "I know a bank where the wild thyme blows" as we touch the wild thyme banks we brought to light while we pinch the green leaves to release the scent. Our last discovery is that from cluttered Burren wilderness we have but liberated the other kind of Burren of rock gardens where its wild flowers grow with now our

"…daffodils

That come before the swallow dares and take

The winds of March with beauty…" (Shakespeare)

April 1990

Shortly after 7 am following an April night of heavy frost, I watched from my window a robin on the top branch of a greening hawthorn, a pair of blackbirds on our Moher flagstones, six starlings on electric wires. Every few minutes they stretched out their wings, letting the sun warm them. Much later there were flashes of gold against blue sea and sky, against fresh green and the greys of our drystone wall – two goldfinches in aerial courtship. Some days later we were caught in a gentle, fine rain, in full sunlight while walking hills on the way to Boston. Though I am not tall I had to stoop to enter a hazel wood. The trees grew thick from moss-covered rocks and gold barred light made vivid violets set in green. Everything seemingly shifting in a steamy haze, a rainforest in microcosm! And these were the kind of woods found on our island, and indeed in Britain, over eight thousand years ago. Some of the limestone rocks supporting us must have been built through aeons by deposits of seashell. Days later as we walked the Rine right out to the furthest limit in Ballyvaughan Bay we saw new deposits flung in heaps by the February/March gales, some whole shells, most ground almost to the consistency of salt. One day we timed the underwater dive of a great northern diver at two and a half minutes. He could, depending on the depth, have been fishing as deep as sixty-five feet. On another day, further from the shore, were four pairs of brent geese upending. Yesterday, some distance out from the rocks, was a flotilla of razorbills, moving their heads sideways, some swimming rapidly within the flotilla and suddenly disappearing in a dive only to re-emerge with necks upstretched. It was a display we'd never before seen. On with the sea concert, "let joy be unconfined"! (Byron).

April 1994

We have been warned – those of us who live in Ireland's western world! Doctors have cautioned against sunburn and sunbathing without a barrier cream. The air is so pure here, they say, that it is unable to filter the skin cancer-causing sun. In most other areas of the planet pollution and smog act as barriers. One pure, unalloyed region and there is a huge fly in the ointment. To be judicious we haven't had much sun since the last week in November 1993! This April day of sunshine, still Atlantic waters, soft spring breezes cast the mildest of spells on birds, creatures of the wild and ourselves. Tons of sand have been pitched up on the Rine during the almost ceaseless winter storms. Each springing grass leaf glitters, polished jade against golden sand crystals. Brent geese and oystercatchers preen themselves while dippers, eternally busy, rush here and there and curlews stalk slowly, pausing occasionally to excavate some delicacy with their long curved bills.

All, however, was not well in our attic. Our clever electrician, a young, strong man, a great player of our gaelic games, climbed up to wire for extra lights. After a few minutes he scuttled down the ladder, white-faced, "Something flew at me." We climbed up and shone torches all over – nothing. Our electrician finished and departed. I ventured up to the attic several times afterwards – nothing. About six months later I saw a piece of fur emerge from a tap. After another six months, just recently, our excellent plumber came to check everything. He showed me what he had found in the attic, in the water system. At the bottom of his red plastic bucket was a drowned pipistrelle bat – fur brown/red, lighter coloured underneath, the face and ears almost black. At six centimetres wide it is about the same size as our smallest mammal, the pygmy shrew and it certainly frightened our six-foot tall electrician! Our poor little bat "hath flown his cloister'd flight" (Shakespeare) and will no more "With short shrill shriek" flit "by on leathern wing". (Collins).

April 1997

The waiting was long, very long but unlike Beckett's Godot it finally came and, except when clouds obtruded, was perfectly visible from mid March to the present. On a recent April night I set my alarm for 3.30 am, sallied forth and sat on a rock in our front field. Straight across and above Galway Bay shone Hale-Bopp, our 'resident' comet, its tail bright though its light was diffused. The hours were full of quietness, no ships moved upon the waters, no cars sped through the stillness. The comet itself seemed immobile and quite near though I knew it was travelling at 27 miles per second and was 123,000 miles away. When more than two thousand years ago it last shone upon the Burren the bards, druids, Celtic chieftains with their well developed and generally humane Brehon laws, their poetry, song, music and craftsmen, held sway. Farmers, fishermen,

hunters and housewives went about their daily lives and all of them must have seen this comet and, like me, wondered. Perhaps they were afraid and took remedies against the comet's awful power. According to Brendan McWilliams in the *Irish Times* when Halley's comet appeared in 1910 people bought comet pills from the then entrepreneurs! Hale-Bopp came with our spring, presiding over a gentle March and April, full of sun, sweet air, primroses, violets, furze, pear, apple and plum blossoms.

Recently I walked by a small, simple church where there must have been a post-Easter wedding – a few shreds of confetti and white artificial flowers lay by the steps. As I stood looking two rooks dropped by. One immediately began scraping up wet leaves. The other picked one of the artificial flowers. Off they flew together, the white flower dangling from the great strong beak – one nuptial to another, one nest-making to another and the white flower and leaves recycled! "Rooks in families homeward go" (Hardy). Perhaps Lady Rook wore a white flower in her head-feathers!

May 1988

And now glory succeeds glory, as light reigns throughout these long western days. This year, because of an especially mild winter followed by a warm, sunny April with sufficiently frequent rain, flowers and plants bloom almost two weeks early. So, as glory descends from the sky, in light and warmth and moisture, so also from the earth glory ascends and we experience again and again the joy of discovery, the delight in each miracle of growth, the first primrose, the first perfect early purple orchid. In grassy spaces, backed by grey/white rocks, we find primroses, violets, purple orchids, the vivid blue of the first gentians, with swathes of mountain avens while, in the hedges, the wild fuchsia stands tall. April and May are the kindest of months. Beyond one of these miniature and unique wild gardens we sighted, on different days a curlew standing on a rock, his slim, long beak upstretched to the sun and a lone great northern diver sitting on the ocean for the fifteen minutes we watched. Our garden and fields resonate with birdsong. Among our hazel, blackthorn, now finished blooming and whitethorn, weighted with blossom, we have nesting blackbirds, robins, chaffinches and, we suspect and hope, goldfinches, wrens and throstles. Today, on a huge Burren rock about ten feet from our kitchen window, we saw two goldfinches. They stayed almost five minutes. My father, a great admirer and with an immense knowledge of wild birds, held that the breast of the male chaffinch blushed deeper in breeding time. We find it plausible since he is a partner in bringing into our world such glory: "He hath a daily beauty in his life." (Shakespeare). Here, each day, we recapture the glory and the joy in discovery, renewing the very essence of childhood – wonder.

May 1990

On an afternoon of light rain between two fine spells we look across our bay at where our Burren hills ought to be. Now they are in a caul of mist. Gradually the light thins, turning the grey darkness to pewter until Ballyvaughan Bay is all silver. On the hills, now visible, the sun strikes to life the green oases seemingly surrounded by glittering metallic shields, limestone slabs still drenched, while the air's moisture sparkles. The Burren is born again. Out from land ventures a ship, slowly sailing. It reminds me of the sheer, almost exquisite intricacy of the old sailing ships, a reminder all the more forceful since I was recently making a model of the original 1779 *USS Constitution*. Being the very proud granddaughter of a man who sailed the seven seas, the youngest commodore captain on one of the great Liverpool lines, together with such model making, brings the realisation that knowledge of a mere rope's function allied to the perfection of its making was a wonderful demonstration of skill and fine control. To live on this storm ripped coast stresses immeasurably the frailty of that very expertise.

Primroses, violets, mountain avens, spring gentians and early purple orchid.

Later on our hill walk we see, beneath foaming hawthorn, close to primroses, violets and mountain avens, a cluster of spring gentians right beside an early purple orchid. Never had we seen them so close to each other, and, while not of the order of lion and lamb lying down together, it is a small miracle. Suddenly two kestrels appear riding the air, one chasing the other, so low they loop that the barred and fanned out tails are visible. Again they climb and then wind-hover away,

"Brute beauty and valour and act
    oh, air, pride, plume, here
    Buckle." (Hopkins).

Twilight thickens and sun and moon sail the sky together while towards a hazel thicket a flock of

"...pigeons make
Ambiguous undulations as they sink
Downward to darkness, on extended wings."
(Wallace Stevens).

May 1991

Storm raged through 5th April. We woke early to see a French factory ship, *Capitaine Pleven II*, grounded on the jagged rocks of *Oileán Lugha* (Illaunloo Island). We watched through field glasses, in our safe house, as each man, sometimes swaying wildly in the gusts, was raised from deck to hovering helicopter. The whole village of Ballyvaughan breathed a sigh of relief when the last man was lifted off. Proud we were of the real bravery and skill of the young servicemen of both our countries – Air Corps from Shannon and the RAF from Brawdy, with Galway lifeboat standing by – who co-operated in saving lives. It was not, however, the end. The rescue complete, the ship still remained on the rocks, listing terribly, with three holes beneath its waterline and aboard over 600 tonnes of oil and 55 tonnes of frozen fish. The danger was obvious – would

Grounded factory ship.

our bay be polluted? The threat lay broadside a mile out, plainly visible, breached, in most turbulent waters. There followed weeks of repair work, all the time being monitored by the Air Corps helicopter, a naval ship and the Pollution Operation Group. In jeopardy were the livelihoods of fishermen, shellfish farmers and the carers for visitors. For who would come not to what they knew to be one of the world's unsullied regions but to one polluted by oil and rotten fish? Co-operation between salvage business and environmental controllers saved the bay. Their activities banished to other areas of the bay, the Rine seals and cormorants from their Illaunloo breeding grounds. As Gogo in *Waiting for Godot* says, "No more weeping," to be answered by Didi, "Perhaps it's not the season"!

The warmth of May surrounds primroses, violets, early purple orchids and spring gentians. In this warmth under a blue sky we walked in a newly discovered part of the Flaggy Shore behind *Cnoc* and *Lios an Bhoirnín*, a beech wood – so unusual in our almost treeless Burren. The leaves gleamed tenderly green over swaying wildflowers. Our seals and cormorants will return, we hope.

"Be still
    Wait." (Roethke).

May 1992

Lament, gentians of spring, eagles. I do not often write of doom and gloom – because there is plenty of both. Several times recently we walked the Burren by Mullaghmore, that

Mullaghmore

21

solitary mountain sweep. We watched the extraordinary swirls of green in Loch Gealáin under the great whorls of limestone, shading from white to blue to violet, delicate and pure beneath sheering winds and sun stroked sky. If ever there were a place to be alone, to capture that harmony which wild beauty and art can give, this is it. And what is to happen here, to the narrow roads whose verges are lined with primroses, violets, cowslips and orchids? The roads are to be widened so that lead belching cars and diesel spouting coaches may travel to the prospective car parks near the soon to be built 'interpretive centre'. All this is planned by our Office of Public Works in St. Stephen's Green, Dublin, with the help of EEC funds, and against all advice from environmentalist organisations. This unique Burren faces so many threats, rare plant stealing visitors, land reclamation, stupid bureaucracy, greed.

Our first sighting of the early purple orchid was early April, of the spring gentians, 18th April in a patch of grass by the sea. On the Doorus peninsula we thought we saw a pair of avocets, frightened into flight by our arrival in a lonely cove. And now for some good news. Maeve and Ailill have taken up residence on Inishvickillaun, one of the Blasket Islands off the Kerry coast. They are *iolar mara*, sea eagles, or in another even more poetic Irish name, *iolar súil na gréine* – 'eagle with the sun's eye'. It is hoped they will breed so that they may join that chain of being, broken one hundred and fifty years ago when the last of them in this region died. It speaks ill of our society that they are to soar, live and have their being on an island privately owned and therefore barred to the general public. May they flourish in their realm,

"Soil, air, water quicken
a word in the seed." (Micheal O'Siadhail)

May 1996

Lost in the Burren! Mullaghmore mountain reared pale, almost white. Its upward sweeping ridges in shade and therefore prominently delineated. Its dramatic quality enhanced by the turlough, Loch Gealáin, shimmering and sparkling in the sunshine. We began to walk 'the round' by Loch Sceath Ard (lake of the high hawthorn) and Loch Trá Bhán (lake of the white strand), keeping Mullaghmore in sight. All was well until we decided to take a shortcut – adventure beckoned, even the unknown! We veered off on to a lane, which led us to a house. We asked if we might walk their back fields and were gladly given permission. For about a kilometre we walked a well-trodden path, which then petered out leaving us smack against a high stone wall. This we managed to scale. Now we had lost all sight of Mullaghmore. Our next obstacle was what looked like an impenetrable hazel wood. However on close examination we noticed various trails. We each took a different one. After a while we met exactly at our starting point! We were faced with a maze of hazel, their long winter catkins, pale lime gold to brown, now fallen. We had to bend double to move on. We passed through small clearings in the hazel woods, here the Burren rocks were moss covered, vividly green, sheltering bouquets of primroses and violets. Brambles tore at us, hazel twigs snapped against us. I thought of 'a hazel switch for the discovery of buried treasure' and its use by the Celtic chieftains as a symbol of their status, stressing their connection to the world of nature. Blackthorn stabbed us, its white flowers like crystals on its black branches – a magnificent year for it. Clouds raced across the sky while we trod on, snail like. A fine mist seeped down as the sun disappeared. At last – the top of Mullaghmore. We had a three-hour creep instead of a two-hour walk!

May 1997

I stood gazing at a doline, a rounded hollow caused by the erosion and collapse of the limestone before the ice age. Everywhere I looked brought the sense of great antiquity – the scratches on the limestone pavements made by the moving glaciers. The very limestone of the Burren was once mud submerged under a tropical ocean over 300 million years ago. I thought of the climates the Burren had endured, tropical, icy, moderate – the variety. And indeed our Burren is a place of variety, not merely during past aeons but today. The surface is a mixture of farmland, hazel groves, great flat stony stretches and rocky hills, sometimes terraced, like Cappanawalla. Turloughs are visible as lakes in rainy weather and as arid hollows in dry spells. The mind travels forward in time with here an ancient ringfort, souterrain, ruined tower house, church, abbey or voyages backwards with there an abandoned 'big house', a deserted stone village, a wedge tomb, a *fulacht fiadh* (cooking site). Even beneath the surface there is variety, hollows, caves, streams, rivers and seawater.

After this ruminative walk I returned to my hacking and there's a great deal to be said for it. Not computer hacking but cutting down brambles, bracken and ivy in a woody area near our dry-stone boundary wall. The bracken has threaded its over-eight-feet way through the trees while the brambles have criss-crossed upwards more than twelve feet. Thoughts of the restoration of the 'Lost Gardens of Heligan' in Cornwall assail me! I was struck by the variety of bird song, robin, blackbird, and thrush above me. Nearby, at wood edge at my feet, were early purple orchids, gentians, violets and primroses. I thought that next year, if all is well and our planting succeeds, they will be joined by bluebells and windflowers – just to increase the variety. For, as Samuel Johnson says, "The joy of life is variety"!

May 1999

I am standing on a limestone clint, a stone wall in front. To my left, on rough grass, primroses, oxlips, cowslips, violets and early purple orchids flourish in the fresh May evening under an almost full moon. Further left the ocean slips against the rocks and to my right Cappanawalla hill, its rounded top brushed with lunar light seems to soar. That was the scene last night as I gazed at the moon trying, without any kind of instrument, to distinguish its lines and configurations. This moon gazing in our Burren night was caused by Dr Philip Stook, a planetary cartographer of the University of Western Ontario, Canada, who also works with NASA. In the *Journal for the History of Astronomy*, with an account given in the *Irish Times* by Kevin

O'Sullivan, he connects the dark semi-circular shapes on the moon with the neolithic carvings on the walls of the passage tombs at Knowth, Co. Meath. Up to Dr Stook's discovery the first lunar map was deemed to be that of Leonardo da Vinci in 1505 AD. However, after much research into Egyptian, Greek, Roman and Chinese civilisations, including neolithic carvings, he claims that the first maps of the moon were made about five thousand two hundred years ago, over four and a half thousand years before Leonardo, and that they are carved on the walls of Knowth. On his own sketch of the moon with its markings he superimposed a copy of a Knowth carving. The match was exact. In a flash of poetic insight the doctor tells us that perhaps when the full moon shines on the best of the Knowth maps "it shines on a map of itself". So I look at our lovely Burren with new eyes, with new respect for its equally ancient neolithic monuments, connected as they are in time, beauty and knowledge to the great alignments of France's Carnac, to the stone Hurlers of Cornwall, to Stonehenge and our own Knowth, Dowth and Newgrange. "Only connect" as Forster says. So we connect to the past becoming a little part of the neolithic age, a little part of a non-primitive people!

View from Cappanawalla mountain.

June 1988

A hare among the gentians, a stoat by a dolmen – we were lucky to see, quite close, these two animals. On our way up Cappanawalla we stopped to rest by one of the Burren's miniature gardens: gentians, cranesbills and mountain avens among rocks veiled by burnet roses. Quite suddenly a large hare, supposedly bigger in the Burren than elsewhere in Ireland, emerged from behind a rock and sat among the flowers. It's all-white tail contrasting with its reddish coat and indicative of its Arctic ancestry. We were afraid to breathe but must have made some movement, for our hare turned its head, gazing at us unalarmed for several seconds. If a hare could be said to amble, ours then ambled off. We watched its progress until it began to run exceedingly fast, probably at its maximum speed of forty miles per hour. Days later, on limestone pavements, a stoat 'accompanied' us to Poulnabrone Dolmen, the sun gleaming on its red-brown coat and creamy underbody, in its mouth a dead mouse. It was quite unafraid of us, taking but a minor interest in our doings. It disappeared down a gryke near the dolmen. This reminded me of a fight between a stoat and a brown rat, which my mother and I witnessed fifty years ago

Wren having a shower.

near my hometown, New Ross. We were sure the bulkier rat would win. As readers will know it did not. The stoat bit the back of its opponent's neck, instantly killing the rat and dragged its body up, through and over the hedge. The victory went to aggression combined with grace, speed, even elegance. We felt, after our meetings with hare and stoat, proud of being looked at by these creatures. After all we had gazed at them!

June 1990

Early mornings bring their rewards. I drove at 6 am by open moor and scrub dotted with hazel groves. On a straight stretch a male merlin, grey-winged, blackbird size, flew in front about two feet from the ground, between the stone walls, for almost a hundred yards. Then it veered, skimming the wall, and disappeared. On another morning as I sat at my desk I gazed across at a hawthorn tree, weighted with blossom and with rain from one of our few recent showers which relieved a dry spell. A wren perched on a branch, tail up. Suddenly it raised its head, pulled with its beak on an overhead twig, stretched out its wings and beat them. These actions were repeated and when I examined them through field glasses I discovered that the wren was seemingly having a shower. When water ran out

Burren hare.

it hopped to another branch and started all over again. Early one Sunday morning we walked the Burren Way, past Rathborney River, past the ringforts of the son of Taidhg, of the Cat and of the Silk (translations of old Irish/Gaelic names), through the fields and meadows up Cappanawalla. Dew lay light on trefoil, bladder campion, vetch, gypsy rose, milkwort (used to kill warts long ago), dog rose, cranesbill, early purple orchids, spotted orchids, marguerites and, on the limestone pavements, burnet roses with their exquisite scent. When we reached the top, through the narrow gap, Ballyvaughan Bay, intensely blue, appeared and beyond it the stretch of Galway Bay with the Twelve Pins (or Bens) of Connemara sharp blue against a paler blue sky. Then climbing from the opposite direction came thirty schoolboys and all of them from my hometown, New Ross in the East of Ireland. Their young voices mingled with the insistent calling cuckoo but, trilling high above them all, Shakespeare's "...lark at heaven's gate" sang or, as Chaucer would have it, "The bisy larke, messenger of day".

June 1996

Our neighbour, Patsy, during the winter and early spring, had made a track up to the top of Cappanawalla mountain (1,024 feet). So that when the cattle are on the mountain in the winter he could, if necessary, bring them fodder and transport a sick or injured animal down quickly as they can twist a foot in the grykes. Patsy tries to farm in the traditional Burren way, sending his cattle up the mountain in winter and bringing them down in summer – the opposite of the Swiss. He asked us if we'd like to climb the new track and we accepted gladly. Off we set, noting the hazel and blackthorn growing almost horizontally in exposed parts, beaten flat by the wind. In the more sheltered areas the hazel stood erect but low with the holly and sometimes an isolated rowan tree. Always there were the Burren rocks and between them patches of grass, sweet and wholesome. On the clints were the saucer-like depressions filled with wild goat droppings. These, some day, will become pockets of fertile soil bearing grass and perhaps a spring

gentian, an orchid or mountain aven. A few fields away we saw the wild goats, shaggy with horns of marvellous size and curvature. At the top we gazed on the fertile valley below, the sea washing gently against its shore. The sky was clouded but the light etched every detail so that each wave of the sea and of the breeze-rustled grass created a unity of movement in our stillness. In the grykes we found maidenhair fern, on grass spaces between the rocks were clusters of spring gentians beside early purple orchids. We descended to the lane, filled with hawthorn, a shrub never to be disturbed, being the fairies' tree and often their home! If cut it bleeds and fairy revenge will be terrible! Therefore it is never picked to decorate the home.

June 1997

To rise here in the Burren at 4.30 am is to be amazed at the amount of light on land and sea and it's good to beat the sun to its rising, about an hour later! On such a morning Mary Ann saw our cat being chased by a badger cub. On another such morning I set off along the Black Head road to examine the hedges. And what a delight they were! Apart from the tall trees and bushes, ash, spindle, hazel, holly, alder, rowan and fuchsia, were their saplings below, six to twelve inches high, erect above the moss and fern beds, alternating with climbing vetch, herb robert and speedwell.

"Quite over-canopied with luscious woodbine,
  With sweet musk roses, and with eglantine" (Shakespeare). I sat on a stile leading down to the Rine and the sea and watched the sun, ruby coloured, rise above the martello tower across the bay on the Flaggy Shore. The waters became streaked with vermilion and all around me a faint rose tint suffused the lovely old limestone walls. In nooks of the old walls and in the hedges were miniature pocket miracles. Chelsea Garden Show could not do better! In one moist, shady place, growing from a cushion of moss, were hart's tongue, brittle bladder, rusty back ferns and, bending over them, maidenhair spleenwort and a few tendrils of herb robert, called *eireaball rí* (erbil ree) in Irish, (king's tail)! I continued my walk, turned a corner, and saw a

beautiful fox leap the hedge. He stood, I stood, gazing at each other. He then, without haste, jumped the opposite hedge leading to Cappanawalla mountain. Ahead of and behind me stretched the hedges, "linear forests" or as Wordsworth puts it,

"These hedgerows, hardly hedgerows, little lines
 Of sportive wood run wild."
I mused upon the loveliness of our islands
 "And the round ocean and the living air".

Miniature garden.

June 1999

Perfection arrived – a June day of blue sky and blue still sea as we departed for the village of Carron, climbing to about two hundred and seventy metres. From Cróide na Bóirne (heart of the rock) we gazed down at the course of the Castletown River and at the biggest turlough in Europe. We recalled the story of a young farmer new to the life who put his sheep into a dry turlough to graze. It rained heavily during the night and next morning the turlough was full of water and poor drowned sheep. Then we retraced our route to Deelin Beg, taking the path to Poulaphuca (the hollow of the puca – Puck in Shakespeare's *Dream*). At last we arrived, breathless, at the magnificent wedge tomb (2000 BC) where all separated to have our own thoughts. The flowerless petals of primroses, violets were everywhere beside spotted orchids, milkweed and burnet roses. The rocky ground with its grass patches shows the wedge tomb off to perfection yet, in the post-glacial period before the first human settlements all this area was, like the rest of our Burren, tree-covered – pine, hazel, yew, perhaps even elm and oak. The tomb, ironically, is the proof of habitation. It is difficult not to wonder at the degree of sophistication of the settlers – a rather arrogant wonder. Their tomb is beautifully crafted and probably their religious ceremonies were equally elegant. All about are cahers (ringforts) some with souterrains (underground chambers) for food storage, dating from 200 BC. A closer look at the terrain down to the valley suggests terracing and indeed when I mentioned this to a UK visitor and *Guardian* reader, Paul Carter, he confirmed that what I took to be terracing was in fact Famine relief work. For what purpose we can only wonder. As Quince says in the Prologue to *Midsummer Night's Dream* "But wonder on, till truth make all things plain." And surely a kind of dream-state is induced while gazing down into one of the Burren's lovely valleys and over to Cnocán na Spáinneach, (the sling of the Spaniard). What gave rise to this name? Who was the Spaniard? How did

Famine relief work at Poulaphuca.

he find himself in this landscape? Did he ever exist? Was he with his sling the figment of imagination and what outward-looking human being named the place? We are in a world bound to language. So, "Gentles, perchance you wonder at this show." (Shakespeare).

July 1989

It is now orchid time here in the Burren. On our walks in this long, hot spell, we see pyramidal, O'Kelly's, fragrant orchids and *Dactylorhiza majalis*. Later, in one of the boats of Aran, the currach, tarred canvas between us and the unfathomed ocean, we rush seemingly straight towards a great, grey stone wall, barren and terrible in its isolation. I remember arriving at Inis Oírr by steamer in 1961 to see a cow, held by its horns at the back of a currach, swimming out to the ship, being hoisted aboard by a crane. Everyone gazed up until warned, "Would ye mind now and not be underneath the beast for 'tis showered ye'll be with primroses and violets." Today, the same grey stone wall is seen for what it is, terraces of grey walls dividing the fields as, on Inis Mór, we climb to Dún Aonghasa on its 270 foot high cliff edge and later as we revisit Celtic crosses, ruined 6th to 15th century churches.

There is a dignity to the islanders that is special. Perhaps it comes from their closeness to and humility towards elemental sea winds. I think of Mrs Conneely, her late husband, Coley and Aunt Mary. The islands affect non-islanders. I think of Bob and Carol Kaske from Cornell University in the United States. Aran brought out all their lovely openness to and humility before a brave community, still epitomising an ancient civilisation. Their visit drove us to read together that truly tautly beautiful tragedy set on Aran, Synge's *Riders to the Sea*. For anyone open to Aran's three islands the words of Synge's character, Maurya, will echo forever, "wind is raising the sea, and there was a star up against the moon, and it rising in the night." The prose lifts, falls with sea, wind and the old language, Irish, spoken so purely and beautifully by the islanders.

July 1990

On the 3rd July we walked from near Fanore towards Black Head on pockets of springy sheep-cropped grass between flat limestone slabs. We came upon miniature flowerbeds, some of purple and crimson cranesbill, cream mountain avens, still sparsely flowering, and yellow pimpernel. Other beds have pink spotted orchids, purple thyme, yellow lady's bedstraw and pink moss campion. Beneath was the sea, calm and, like the sky, deep blue. In the middle distance the three Aran Islands were distinct. A yacht was "scintillant in the minute brilliance" of this cloudless day. A flash of reddish brown betrayed the presence of a young stoat which, with wonderful agility, fled to the drystone wall and watched us from a gap with its bright eyes, shining nose and round ears alert. Later in the evening, with the aid of field glasses, I was able to identify a dunnock and a cuckoo side by side on electricity wires. Every few minutes the dunnock would turn its head to the cuckoo, which immediately called "cuckoo". An unfortunate deceived parent? In a sense I now take with me on my walks our *Guardian* readers, some of whom have written so beautifully of the land and nature they love – some I've even met!

The fourth of July dawned, a mixture of sun and rain. As we returned early from Ballyvaughan village we saw from base to midway of Cappanawalla mountain a great band of rainbow with sun streaming above it. Later on a short walk up the lane to Newtown Castle we noted roses growing in the hedges: dog roses, pink tinged with slightly arched stems, cream wild roses, yellow, green centred sweet briar, its petals shaded from almost white to pink edges. We encouraged each other to smell the roses but discovered no scent remained after a single sniffing! Shortly afterwards the rain came, "With hey, ho, the wind and the rain" (Shakespeare) but

"The rainbow comes and goes,
  And lovely is the rose." (Wordsworth).

July 1991

Although we have walked by sea, up hills, in country lanes seeing one stoat, a few hares, the majority of our wildlife sightings have been at home. One day of warmth and sun on the Flaggy Shore we saw a pair of shelducks and later we sat and watched two simultaneous aerial displays: terns over dunes and rocks, swallows over road and grass, "all air and nerve", scaling,

Lizards.

riding, diving through currents. We had to leave. How long did these displays last – all eighteen hours of our long western daylight? Nearer home, the cormorants have returned after being frightened off by the activity in removing the factory ship from the rocks in April, but the seals are not back yet. Twice we saw 'our' pine marten, once running on our stone wall and then crossing our drive after eating wild strawberries. On another day I saw, in shade by a doorstep, a viviparous lizard, black on green, the skin delicately geometrically scaled. I was about to shoo it into sunlight when a slight movement arrested me. Another lizard, longer – about five inches – the female, on the wall. I retreated hastily. Two chaffinches, tamer than our robin, undisturbed from their breadcrumbs by our clatterings, reached catastrophe. Mary Ann called and I came running. The female chaffinch had crashed into glass and lay little feet in the air. I held her in my hand to warm her, feeling her small heart thud, rapidly at first then steadily. Mary Ann held water to its beak. All the while the mate, on a hazel tree, chittered. After forty minutes I placed her on a rock. The male flew to her and, to our wonder, held himself poised over her, chittering, scrabbling with his feet until he succeeded in moving her to a grass hollow. Soon she looked perky. Thirty minutes later they both flew off. A friend witnessed a large dog attack a nanny goat grazing with cattle. One of the cows tried to save the goat. The dog was put down, the goat survived. Manifestly it's not always "nature, red in tooth and claw".

July 1993

Once upon a time, a very short time ago, we were sitting, chatting to our French friend, Stéphane, in our grianán (sunroom) at the back of our house. Threads of darkness were beginning to embroider the light of our long western evening while we sat in comfort, with the limestone pavements and rocks of the Burren glowing pure and silver grey all around us. Honeysuckle, apricot coloured, edged with claret, trailed over the rocks and over the hollows white burnet roses foamed. The air was fragrant, the honeysuckle giving off its strongest

Pine marten - cat crainn.

perfume at this time of day. It was very quiet, "All the air a solemn stillness holds" (Gray). Suddenly Stéphane put her finger to her lips... there he was, brown suited, honey coloured front, quite at home. He lolloped down from the back and towards us, uninvited but so welcome. We remained silent, nearly immobile, except for slow, measured almost ritualised movements when we turned to keep track of him. He was, of course, *Martes martes*, our Burren pine marten. His fur, richly brown, was thick and long, that on the tail even more so. In the evening's slanted light he was glossy, burnished. Now and again he stopped to snuffle under the earth for slugs and snails. At last he came to the rock where we throw crumbs for the birds – no more than five feet from us. On to this he jumped with supreme agility and began to hoover up the crumbs. We could see distinctly the long claws and the thick fur on the front feet as he faced us. The eyes were large, shining, the round ears fringed with creamy fur. He jumped down from the rock and, *mirabile dictu*, bounded over to the door, ascended the step and looked straight in at us, still frozen in position. Then he turned, not in the least frightened, snuffled in the earth and disappeared. We rushed to the front window and there he was – his head stuck in a clump of heather. The whole episode lasted over thirty minutes, here, "in summer's wonderland". (Noyes).

July 1994

Frog in a gryke and a 'plague'! We, Mary Ann's Californian cousins and ourselves, were walking the clints and grykes beneath lovely whorled Mullaghmore mountain on a day of shifting cloud, intermittent brightness and occasional fine sieved rain. About two feet down a gryke, among clusters of maidenhair spleenwort, brittle bladder fern and wild maidenhair fern, crouched a small dark grey frog. Later we passed a field full of pink spotted orchids, marguerites waving gently above them while below tufts of cranesbill added their vivid dark pink. Further on, by a turlough, shrubby cinquefoil was in flower. On a stretch of at least a mile, on a narrow lane, the 'plague' caught up with us – froglets, hundreds, some as big as three centimetres, most a mere two. It required delicate footwork, World Cup quality! not to tread on them. They were leaping everywhere. Some were pale yellow, some green, yet others light to dark grey.

This danger over another soon loomed. A herd of mother cows and their calves in the laneway. They insisted on preceding us. We stopped at a roadside garden where an elderly lady busied herself and we voiced our fears of driving the cattle further and further from their farm. "Have no fear at all. About a mile on they'll disperse," she said. We chatted to her and, with such natural courtesy, she presented each of us with a flower from her garden, old, sweet smelling roses. A farmer stopped his car, pointed back to the cattle and asked, "Is it to the fair you're driving them?" We were to face yet more 'danger'. A large bull fancied one of the passing cows. He stamped, snorted and made for a five-foot high hedge. He climbed it and padded towards a break in the wall in the next field and so into our lane. We ran – the cows and calves luckily having reached their place of dispersal off our pathway. Such are the hazards of taking a walk in rural Ireland. We had "glory and danger alike"! (Thucydides).

July 1995

We, our five American friends, Mary Ann (professors all) and myself board the small boat for Aran's Inis Meáin, the middle island. Great is the laughing talk on our way across the ruffled ocean, the sky mist-filled, and a bitter little wind tearing at clothes and hats. On arrival, joined by two American students, we make for Dún Chonchúir stone fort high in the island's centre. When we reach its walls of lichen-covered loose stones the sun breaks from the clouds winging their way north and away. We overlook the steep valley sheering down to the west; the fort's northern side set on an inland cliff. Talk ceases. There is only silence, the quiet of space, of airy stillness. A private corner is claimed by each of us, as we contemplate what is eternal on our earth. The beauty of sea, sky and the fort – man's ancient contribution. Archaeologists are now convinced that these so-called forts were in no sense military establishments but were places of pagan ritual. We gaze across at Black Head on the western edge of the Burren, realising that aeons past we could have walked there and from one Aran island to the next, the sea in its everlasting restlessness smashing the limestone connections into sand, pebbles that lie about the ocean floor. Ann and I set out to find *Cathaoir Synge* (Synge's chair) on the western limit of the island. Bloody cranesbill lines the path, colouring pink one small field with its bleached limestone walls. Gradually the path becomes narrower, a donkey's width, the stone walls head-high and soon so high that it is possible to see only through the gaps. We round a bend and there before us is broken ground, cliff-high, with the mighty western ocean below and stretching ahead. Here Synge sat, working out his *Aran Islands* and *Riders to the Sea*. The lovely words of Synge's Maurya hint at Inis Meáin's struggle and survival, "you can hear the surf is in the east, and the surf is in the west, making a great stir with the two noises and they hitting off one another."

Dún Chonchúir, Inis Meáin.

July 1996

The great advantage in leaving the Burren for several weeks is the pure joy of our return. We round the last bend on the hill and see beneath us the wide bay framed by its hills, beautiful in their austerity. Our hearts rejoice. Then we "...welcome, somer, with thy sonne soft" (Chaucer) and, like Chaucer's searchers plan to go on 'pilgrimages'! High in the hills we still find mountain avens and gentians, especially this year because of the late spring. However it is the quest for the wild orchids that recently sent us forth. On a day of blue skies and sea we walked down the lane to O'Loghlen's Castle, checking the nearby fulacht fiadha (ancient cooking place). On reaching the shore, the sun's heat reflecting from the limestone rocks and pavements, we scrambled over boulders, stones, sometimes treading the clints, all the time carefully scrutinising the field edges. At last, among the rocks in a grassy oval bordered with burnet roses are the white orchids. I stopped counting at fifty. On our return by the lane to the Black Head road we noted the intermingling of warm ruby fuchsia with the pale elegance of wild roses. Indeed almost everywhere along road and lane edges grow the spotted orchids. We have them together with the white in our fields. Some orchids I have never seen but this year, thanks to our friends, Doreen and Bernie Comyn, we were lucky. Four of us, pilgrims all on what has now become a rare rain-filled day, tramped along the edge of a summer meadow full of buttercups, then through short grass and there they were, clusters of them. Bee orchids, each tall spike with three, four, five or six blooms and, as the name implies, closely resembling a bumblebee, black and yellow on rich pink petals. Ah! "Hard is the herte that loveth nought in May..." (Chaucer) or in June or July!

July 1998

To return from Wexford County to the Burren is to be again struck with wonder; a different wonder comprising a journey from lush fertility, metres-deep topsoil to a land of stone. To put a spade to make a flowerbed in the Burren is to discover two

centimetres of topsoil – it is fertile – underlaid by rock. How we
have envied the ant in our difficult excavations. The creature
can, I'm told, lift fifty times its own weight! Now I stand
marvelling at thirty wild orchids, twayblades, common spotted,
heath spotted, O'Kelly's and pyramidal. There was intense
excitement here in May when purple gentians were found. I
searched but found none except the Alpine spring blue. I
suspect May's purple gentians were just very dark blue. I have
often found changes in colour here in the Burren, especially
with wild violets and hawthorn berries. However the wonders
are here awaiting discovery. On a recent walk I saw, growing in
a mossy hollow of a stone wall, seven different kinds of fern –
perfect, no gardener could have been more creative.

At four thirty in the morning the sun had almost fully risen
from behind Finavarra peninsula. On an unrippled sea circles
and ellipses of golden light formed burnished pools and not a
straight line to be seen. I mused recalling the flowing lines of
Celtic monastic art – no straight lines. And since the old
monks but continued the more ancient pre-Christian culture I
remembered the swirling rhythms of Newgrange's stone
inscriptions and the rounded ornamentation of Celtic gold
collars. So I returned to the oval heads and elliptical petals of
the thirty orchids, of the moss-bedded ferns. Perhaps we
should erect a curvaceous monument to the inventor of the
straight line who made possible the square and the rectangle!
So at evening's end

   "…the night
   In ever-nearing circle weaves her shade.
   I see her veil draw soft across the day."
   (Matthew Arnold).

August 1988

Peace, poetry, scones and surprises. Today we walked in
Finavarra and by the Flaggy Shore, stopping to gaze at the site
of the ancient 15th century Bardic school. Here, in the Gaelic
era, men served their time, twelve years or more, to the poet's
art, under a bardic master poet. Sitting together at night in

Fireplace in Mount Vernon and detail of tiles (private).

silent darkness composing their lines. Powerful figures they
were, the old Gaelic bards and many a chieftain bit the dust
because of their satire on his behaviour and rule. The bards were
at once feared and loved and always respected. Close by is a
simple monument to one of the last Gaelic poets of the region,
Donncha Mór O'Dálaigh (O'Daly). Here too or nearby wandered
the great Gaelic blind poet, Raftery, much admired later by
Yeats. Raftery wrote a poem on his blindness, *"Mise Raiftearaí an
file…"* in which he describes himself as "full of hope and love".
It would be hard to walk this way, across the limestone
pavements by the rock pools full of muted colour with the great
sea, for the moment, lapping quietly against the rocks, without

experiencing hope for the preservation of beauty and love for its profusion. The harebells are everywhere moving gently in the faint breeze. Further along the shore swallows dip and rise. A flock of starlings sheers off towards the land. At last we arrive at Mount Vernon, formerly the seaside summer home of Lady Gregory of Coole Park, near Gort. One of her ancestors who knew George Washington asked his permission to name this house after Washington's Mount Vernon. So here we pass from the old Gaelic dispensation to Irish poets and dramatists writing in English. Here in Mount Vernon Yeats, George Bernard Shaw, Sean O'Casey and John Millington Synge resided as summer guests of Augusta Gregory. Here she herself, in her little corner overlooking her walled garden, translated the old Irish stories and folklore into English, joining together both languages. Here too Augustus John designed fireplaces for the two front rooms, the actual bricklaying being a communal effort of family and friends. Here now we partake of the present owner's scones at afternoon tea whilst gazing out at the green and ruby fuchsia hedge and through a gap to the front field. Here at high tide the sea enters into a small hollow. This provided a delightful swimming pool for Lady Gregory's grandchildren. Beyond that and the little lane the sea moves like silk across to Aughinish. As Raftery wrote, though in another tongue, "Star of light and harvest sun."

August 1989
At last the heat of the long, light days of June and July, some with eighteen hours daylight, has been dampened by freshening Atlantic rain. Flowers and hedges have lost their dusty look. I call these days the year's 'blue/purple' period. Delicate harebells, tall scabious, knapweed and thistles toss in the gusty winds. Limestone bugle and wild thyme lie low, blues and purples changing hue as sunlight and cloud-light alternate.

  "...Then the sea
   And heaven rolled as one and from the two
   Came fresh transfigurings of freshest blue."
  (Wallace Stevens).

Birds are silent, their feathers dishevelled as they moult. On a Burren rock at ground level, three feet from our glass kitchen door, we put crumbs for the birds. Here, on a morning (6.30 am) of warm light, Mary Ann alerted me to a 'miracle'. A pine marten was eating the crumbs. We decided it was not 'our' large male pine marten, last sighted in June, but probably either one of its young or the smaller female. It had such a youthful look as it snuffled up the crumbs. Its fur, rich chocolate brown on the sides and back was infinitely soft while the cream front had the lustre of satin. It was very cat-like, making me recall its Irish (Gaelic) name, *cat crainn* (cat of the trees). The claws were thick and immensely strong, the eyes very bright and the nose black and shining. But it was its ears that were so alluring, large and oval, the brown delicately edged with cream. We watched it for ten minutes until it had eaten all the crumbs and left its mark. It then walked away, jumped with easy elegance on to a limestone clint and disappeared down a gryke. We know people who watch long hours for a sighting of this beautiful, wild creature and never glimpse it. Once more in this Burren of 'miracles' we were privileged.

August 1992
Ladies, a banana boat, monsters of the deep and a flotilla. Some intrepid ladies of Ballyvaughan, many of them members of the Ballyvaughan Ladies Club, decided to go for a jaunt on the banana boat out into the bay. The banana boat is a long, bright yellow rubber craft with a hump right down the middle on which passengers sit astride. It is towed by a powerboat, the objective being to go fast and to dislodge the riders. Before the trip there was much talk and speculation as to the ladies' staying power, much laughter and fun about the coming adventure. At last the evening arrived and with it lashing rain and grey skies. Off they set, gazed at by our two resident swans and their five cygnets, until the yellow boat was but a speck in the gloom. When the banana boat arrived out in the bay, almost opposite our house, all its riders fell off. To their consternation they re-surfaced to find themselves, as one of

them described it, "in the middle of a school of sharks." In their fright they cried out, "Sharks . . . help . . . HELP." They need have had no fear – the sharks were a school of dolphins who were very happy to have company, continuing quite unperturbed to ride the waves, snuffling as they went. The resident cygnets and parents gazed again at the very wet and laughing ladies on their return to the pier.

By the Claddagh in Galway a few days ago we counted over a hundred swans. Mr Alex Bowlby, writer on World War Two and reader of these diaries, describes what he saw on his return visit to Galway in 1979 as a group of swans sailed by. "The leader was a couple of yards ahead of the rest, who were in line behind, exactly one yard between each. There were two outriders, exactly the same distance from the line and dead level with each other. This was another sort of beauty – the precision, the effortlessness of it beat any Guards on the parade ground."

August 1992 Extra

Recently, before 6 am, the bay of Ballyvaughan, shot with silver, great lustrous spokes reaching from sea surface to streaked and breaking clouds, I set off to survey territory, despite the, as yet, breakfastless Pusscat, left yowling and irritated. As I gazed out to the wide Galway Bay I thought I was seeing things, surely it was a mirage, a ghost. It was, however, no spirit ship, here where in the twelfth and thirteenth centuries Spanish, French and Irish merchantmen plied between Galway and mainland Europe. It was a three-masted ship, top gallants, topmast, lower and jib sails white and full in the luminous grey of sea and sky, "This fabulous shadow only the sea keeps". (Hart Crane). As I watched the grey drained away in the gold of the sun rising which struck the gilded figurehead so that, for a while, the ship sailed in a burnished lough,

"With all her bravery on, and tackle trim,
  Sails fill'd, and streamers waving." (Milton).

Soon the sails were furled and the ship anchored not far off our Rine. It was the Italian training ship the *Palinuro* making for Galway.

I returned to the daily round to see old Pusscat of the weak back legs suddenly stretch out a formidable front paw, clamping on a *dallóg fraoigh* (translation – blind young fury), pygmy shrew, all 5 cms of it including its long whiskered nose. I caught and released it to its frenetic routine of ceaseless foraging. Eating to stay alive, from grass to weed bed to its nocturnal seashore visits. Sandhoppers in the high tide seaweed are caviar to it. Later, Pusscat fed and fast asleep inside, I saw a goldfinch bend a two foot high grass. It did this by starting the bend close to the ground and then tightrope walking along the stem. Truly there's little need to watch the televised Olympics – and how satisfying to see the bird receive the equivalent of a medal when it came to the grass head – a luscious meal!

August 1993

We watched for a long time a pair of herons and a young one stand motionless beside Loch Muirí on Finavarra peninsula while about twenty swans fed further out on the loch, moving at times with such ease that their passage was wake-less. Suddenly, like lightning, one of the adult herons thrust his head forward and down, the piledriver beak knifing something edible, too small for us to distinguish. Neither of the other two birds took the slightest interest, remaining quite still, utterly intent on their own quest. Nearer home, on the flanks of Cappanawalla, under great sheets of Atlantic rain sun-shot so that it swept the hillside in golden showers, illuminating the infinite variety of green and grey, a herd of twenty-four wild goats grazed, two of them on their hind legs reaching into a succulent bush. Some days later, as we walked the exposed limestone pavements of the Rine peninsula we found yet another minuscule golden-sanded beach newly fashioned by the never-ending battering of the mighty tides. Stones and boulders flung aside in movements so careless as to seem almost contemptuous. The tide was halfway in so we had a fine stretch to walk. We were upset to find a beautiful vixen lying dead, evidently recent, the lovely head, body and tail stilled forever. It made us wonder about her cubs and their fate. Some distance away from us, at the end of the Rine, cattle, some honey-coloured others dark red, lay resting. Near them we noticed darker clumps and thought they were piles of kelp or rocks until one of them moved! To our delight they were seals, a small colony. The sea creature and the land animal shall lie together! There is little, I think, except great art, to equal the sense of privileged harmony that results from seeing our fellow creatures in their world. It seems like a regaining of a lost world of unity and peace though I doubt such a world ever existed except in that most powerful element, the imagination! Nature, as Emerson says, "...carves the bow of beauty".

August 1996
Mary Ann and our French visitors, Marie France and Philippe Lacaze, decided to scale the 'heights' of Mullaghmore while I kept to the lowlands to fulfil my wish of walking round the turlough (disappearing lake) at its foot. We had seen from a distance waterlilies on the turlough – these I wished to see up close. Because of dry weather the water had almost disappeared leaving but a few pools so I set off with high hopes and a stout stick to test the ground ahead lest I sink! All seemed easy at first but I soon discovered beneath my feet a veritable constellation of wild flowers and plants. My efforts to avoid treading on them resulted in a walk like that of a drunken sailor, made worse by myriads of disturbed butterflies, moths and leaping frogs. What a paradise! Shrubby cinquefoil, late mountain avens, orchids: deep pink pyramidal, O'Kelly's white, fragrant, purple and pink patches of wild thyme, yellow ladies' bedstraw, maidenhair fern, gold Aztec-headed carline thistles, harebells. However as I got nearer my target, the waterlilies, I realised I could not get close. Rushes grew well over my head and the whole lily-bearing pool was circled by a deep 'moat'. On I

Dragonflies and waterlilies.

trudged, now through shrubby cinquefoil (*Potentilla fruticosa*), now over rocks where hazel grew and spread horizontally. I stopped to examine a hazelnut – pale green, its tip suffused with deep pink. Then I noticed a very small pool. Floating on its surface were four waterlilies and hovering above them dragonflies and damselflies. I also saw two hovering matchstick-like (but thinner) opaque blue, seemingly wingless insects. Annoyingly none of my reference books help me to identify them. I scrambled back in the perfumed air in a cloud of butterflies, matching the darting swallows overhead, so that I did not know whether I was "dreaming I was a butterfly or that I was a butterfly dreaming I was human"! (Chuang Tzu).

August 1997
I looked up through the leaves and flowers of a high wild fuchsia tree at the blue sky. Such a sight – dark green leaves, hanging ruby flowers, young branches all vermilion spread against the clarity of an azure firmament. One of the small simple glories of a walk in our Burren. As Hazlitt said, "Give me a clear blue sky over my head, and the green turf beneath my feet, a winding road before me, and a three hour march to dinner – and then to thinking!" My next stop brought me to an expanse of pink-flowered wild thyme. Erect above were two purple scented orchids, behind rich yellow lady's bedstraw, a little further on high purple-headed knapweed, the whole almost enclosed by the scattered light grey Burren stones. All over this limestone region there are these simple pleasures waiting for the eyes to see. I could see, unlike Keats, "what flowers are at my feet", could smell the thyme intermingled with orchids and lady's bedstraw, so that

"I will be the gladdest thing under the sun!
I will touch a hundred flowers and not pick one!"
(Edna St Vincent Millay).

All was silent as I walked, "no bird sang", it being their time of silence after all the hustle and bustle of feeding and rearing their fledglings – quite worn-out they must be! Peace was, like the blue sky, over all. I descended from the hills to

Ballyvaughan Bay and rested on a rock in a small golden beach I know. A few gulls floated on calm water, slow waves lapped over my feet, three or four oystercatchers foraged among rocks and sand, and I almost fell fast asleep! Then I saw yet another lovely picture – two adult choughs, red curved bills and polished purple-black feathers, beside them their two duller plumaged young ones. After their forage they soared and wheeled away into sea space and sky distance.

Wild thyme, purple scented orchids and lady's bedstraw.

August 1998

Today is wet – very! I am walking in my waterproof gear under a large golf umbrella. The rain flails the earth. Even the water collected on leaf, berry, flower courses in streams. Each hazel leaf is bent, overburdened by water. Rain beats against and off the flowers of hedgerow fuchsia. Fierce gusting winds driving in to sting face and hands. I have to close the umbrella for fear of taking off! The sky is a uniform light grey; the stone walls vary from pale to dark grey, almost black. Sea and hills are invisible. Gloomy – this summer day in August? Not for me. The hedges are full of colour, pink and white wild roses, fuchsia with its ruby and purple flowers, montbretia's flame-like petals, harebells' silken blue, all shaken, propelled into ceaseless motion against an infinity of green shades, soft, pale, dark and all washed so clean, so clear. A robin shelters deep in a holly tree, reminding me of a Clare farmer's protection of a robin and her young. He found her nest in his Massey-Ferguson tractor, near the windscreen and steering wheel. Every second day she laid an egg until there were six. He ensured the family cat couldn't get anywhere near the nest, using the tractor as little as possible although he drove it to his daughter's primary school so that the pupils could see and marvel at the nest and its fledglings. The young birds all survived and in their own time fled their tractor nest. What a grand man! I continue my walk and am lucky to find a cluster of purple scented orchids. I kneel in the wet to sniff their clove-like scent. Such a seemingly small discovery, such delightful wonder! So, in an almost underwater world I plod home with heavy feet and light spirits,

"With a noise of winds…
  With a clamour of waters…" (Swinburne).

August 1999

Breakfast at 7.45 am, sitting at my desk, looking out at the garden and beyond it the sea, whilst I intermittently read *Rodinsky's Room* by Rachel Lichtenstein and Iain Sinclair. A magpie alights on the windowsill, less than a metre away. It gazes in at me with the ever-inquisitive eyes of the crow family and I gaze back, admiring the beauty of its white and black plumage, that black with such a green gloss. Finally it flies off to take its stand on a rock, a natural sculpture. Then suddenly my window space is filled with busy to-ings and fro-ings, loop-the-loops, breathtaking dives and instant turns – swallows now but a metre away. No hide, no other vantage point could provide a closer view. I can see quite distinctly the longer tail streamers of the male, the white bars across the tails, the buff underbodies, some almost ruddy, the blue-black upper wings. The twittering calls crescendo and diminish but never cease. Nothing to do but watch, wonder and so I do, thinking no man-produced Millennium extravaganza could equal this free spectacle! I peer out. The swallows are lined up on the guttering pecking down into it. They are breakfasting too! Truly I can say,

"Sweet is the breath of morn, her rising sweet,
  With charm of earliest birds."
  (Milton).

Later, past Black Head lighthouse, we notice the sea spread like silver chain mail. Then a ruffling, an agitation occurred. Dolphins were barely cresting the water then disappearing. We watched them with lots of summer visitors – all were silent. Perhaps the wonder of a possible bond between human beings and the creatures of the wild struck us. I remembered an incident related to us by our friend Mary Keegan. She was walking the Burren's Flaggy Shore when she noticed a solitary baby dolphin, slightly injured. Mary picked him up in her arms and put him into the sea. He circled and came back. She again immersed him and again he returned. A third time she cradled him and released him into the waters. This time he again circled and circled and then swam out into the bay. The privilege of holding such a marvellous creature and returning it to its natural element was certainly felt by Mary and ourselves.

"And now the Sun had stretcht out all the hills,
  And now was dropt into the western bay."
  (Milton).

September 1992

I watched through field glasses from our house the seals on the Rine. They looked so wonderful that off I tramped to get a closer look. There they were, *Ron Glas* (*Glas:* grey or green), young bulls and cows. What colours, soft grey, mottled with brown, shading to black, the grey almost green in the females – their heads and tails uplifted like bananas. I was spotted and while I remained quite still some of them began to show off by entering the water to submerge and resurface, looking back to see if I was noticing. I noted this delight in display years ago in Cornwall. The others remained beached, now watching me and then the cavortings. Overhead on a dark to pale blue sky whole ranges of clouds, pure white, luminous, opal, sunstruck, golden-edged, moved in majesty. Wind-driven across them, billows of delicate grey, the sea, navy, light blue and shimmering green – a "world of light" and close by "The seal's wide spindrift gaze…"(Hart Crane).

Many mornings recently, following tradition on this west coast, we've gone off to gather seaweed, to be tipped out on our return and left to rot down. In October Mary Ann will have it dug in to the vegetable and flowerbeds. On the day I trotted to see the seals we had fish pie, made from pollock caught in the bay by Dermot and brought to us by his wife Majella and her mother, Maura. With it we had mangetout peas, sown and cultivated by Mary Ann. We've been eating them since the first of July. Sometimes we've had homegrown artichokes. Our failure to produce more than one apple on either of our two trees still rankles! However we must have a mocking bird (!) because the bright red apple on one tree was laid, half-eaten, by our back door! The following morning it was gone, taken by our pine marten whose droppings lay nearby. Our garden has no fairies but, as a woman asked recently if she believed in fairies, replied, "'Deed I don't but they're there."

Seals - hauled out.

September 1994

Three hundred years and more – a long time compared to the
life of an individual yet a mere moment in relation to the
ancient, bare hills, fertile valleys and stark seascape of our
lovely Burren. Over three centuries ago, through mist and
sweeping Atlantic rain, sun shimmering on whitened rock,
poor and rich, walking or riding, intent on learning, they came
to the great O'Davoren Brehon Law School at Cathair Mhic
Neachtain and to the Bardic School at Finavarra. From *ollamh*
(professor) to student the great traditions of Celtic poetry and
law were handed down. In many instances the Brehon laws
were more civilised than any other contemporary system in
Europe. Then in the sixteenth century, equidistant from both
places of learning, a castle was built, today's Newtown Castle,
built for defence – war was not absent.

About six years ago a young man, Michael Greene from
Ballyvaughan in the Burren, had a dream. He and his wife Mary
bought the roofless Newtown Castle. With Mary's brother,
Martin Hawkes and supported by the Hyland family they began
transmuting dream into reality. Local builders and craftsmen
renovated the castle, facing new buildings with Burren stone.
Under the presidency of Professor Eugene Wicks and staff the
first students recently finished their summer courses. We now
have the perfectly equipped, internationally recognised Burren
College of Art in Ballyvaughan. Once again, after three
centuries, there is a seat of higher learning and creativity in the
Burren. A military castle has been transformed into a place of
peace where natural beauty and human creativity interact. The
college was opened by our President, Mary Robinson, no mean
lawyer herself. Her pride in local initiative joined to interna-
tional co-operation, one of her dreams evident. An individual's
lifespan is a mere dream-span but this dream assumes reality in
the very stone, the very rock that is the Burren.

"Only through art can we get outside ourselves and know
another's view of the universe which is not the same as our
own and see landscapes which would otherwise have remained
unknown to us." (Marcel Proust).

Former President Mary Robinson at Burren College of Art.

41

September 1995

Where have all the butterflies gone? I think they were all in our garden at the end of August and into September. There they flitted and fluttered, blues, whites, brimstones, browns, small tortoiseshells and peacocks. Once, after unceasing nectar-tippling on our lavender bushes, the house was invaded by small tortoiseshells. We chased them, flapping our arms and, when near enough, blowing behind them to get them out through the windows – absolutely exhausting! One, I'm happy to say, secreted itself behind a portrait of Mary Ann's ancestor and has started its hibernation. I taped a cardboard likeness on the frame – a reminder not to disturb the creature when dusting. Where do all the butterflies go when it rains? I have often wondered. There was a light shower in the middle of all the tortoiseshell traffic so I investigated. I found some comfortably settled on twigs under umbrellas of layered hazel leaves; others in holes in our dry stone walls – all with their wings folded together.

A startling visitor touched down at Shannon Airport, Co. Clare, at the end of August. It lodged on the lagoon at the nearby hotel. Its colour was as bright, its form as strange as anything that disembarked from the planes – a flamingo. Surely it came to cheer the Clare team in the All-Ireland Hurling Final – they won! Parents and two fledgling swallows rested by our roof guttering. The adults chased away our resident wagtail when he alighted close by. What a summer with Mary Ann's home grown broad beans, sugar-snap peas, haricots verts, courgettes and tomatoes. A few rainy spells, short-lived showers since 13th June – autumn gliding in with blue skies, warmth and wind-stilled days. On the summit of Aillwee mountain we walk for hours – field scabious and harebells stretching to purple heather above limestone pavements blanched with sun. Below, the bay reaches the ocean's blue immensity, an unruffled sea gently edging the rocks and coastal fields. "Brightened with joy" (Wordsworth) we turn for home.

Sheltering butterflies.

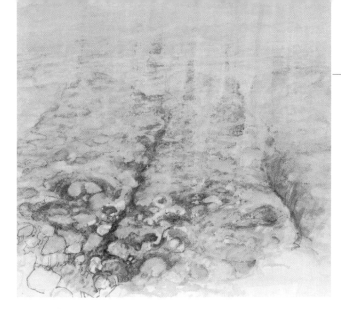

The Flaggy Shore.

September 1996

I am sitting on a limestone pavement by the Flaggy Shore writing this diary in my head. My hand lies on a crinoid, the fossil of an ancient sea lily. The day is calm, not a wrinkle on the sea. It barely moves against the rocks, beneath it seaweed wavers gently. Light rests on the surface, a gleaming silver illumination with not the slightest glare. From this watery mirror it reflects back to land and air, rendering the one darker in texture, the other lighter in tone. The sky itself, originator of this silver transformation, holds manifold shades, multiple lightnesses. A world of chiaroscuro, at once lustrous and shadowy. No sound crashes upon the silvern quietness yet the very air seems to resonate, the soft sheen to be somehow sonorous. Truly

"Heard melodies are sweet, but those unheard
  Are sweeter." (Keats).

Slowly life manifests itself. A few gulls appear overhead, wings spread, tipped with silver light. A sea snail with silvered whorls edges forward in the rock pool beside me. Light spreads upon the limestone pavements, their saucer depressions, fringed with salt, shine and gleam like frost rime. Softly, slowly rain falls, silver drops in an undiminished light. Puncture points roughen the sea and, as the shower becomes heavier, the drops hit and rebound so that it seems to be raining both down and up. The air fills with a faint drumming. Limestone turns from silver to lead. Water runs everywhere, movement and activity encompassing shore and sea. Drops become droplets and then cease. All is argentine again until golden rays disperse throughout, momentarily invading this silver world. The sun makes prominent the greenness of the grass and the intense colour of silken-textured harebells, each five-lobed flower like a blue star as I look into its centre. The wonderful harebell, enticing insects to pollinate but, when they do not oblige, self-pollinating. A day

"Enwrought with gold and silver light." (Yeats).

September 1997

The Burren and Kinvara. I wondered how they felt, what they thought when they arrived from France in the late seventeen hundreds to settle along the Claddagh in Kinvara. To worship in the small Huguenot church erected by them, the site of which I now gazed at. It surely must have been strange to hear French spoken amid the Irish language, stranger still as a minority to be free to worship while the Catholic majority had to wait over a century for a similar liberty. The Huguenots of Kinvara must have prospered for in 1760 they built Delamaine Lodge, a beautiful Georgian cottage close to Kinvara Bay. William Delamain married Hannagh O'Shaughnessey, the daughter of a local chieftain. Later the Delamain wealth was greatly increased by smuggling during Napoleonic times, illegal export of wool being exchanged for equally illegal imports of brandy, wine and tobacco. Of course, a secret tunnel was supposed to run from the Lodge to the shore to facilitate matters. William and Hannagh's son re-emigrated to France where he married the daughter of a cognac merchant in Jarnac. What a busy place Kinvara must have been, sail-making, boat building, blacksmithing, thatching and markets. The little seaport boasted at least five hotels. As I stood by the sea between Kinvara and its Dunguaire Castle I saw seaweed loaded

Kinvara in the late 1700s.
1. Delamaine Lodge 2. The Claddagh 3. Huguenot chapel, built 1782.

on a trailer. This gathering of seaweed for fertiliser has lasted for centuries. Once a raft, a *climín*, was made of it. A man then stood on it, floating it ashore with a pole. Near the seaport lie the limestone rock and hills of the Burren where, on my return, I found a creamy burnet rose and a cluster of oxlips late blooming among the blue harebells. So later "when it came night, the white waves paced to and fro in the moonlight, the wind brought the sound of the great sea's voice to us" on shore. (Stephen Crane).

September 1998
Up past Rathborney River, before it descends into the earth to become one of the Burren's underground rivers, past Lios na gCat (Ring of the Cat), Feenagh, Gleninagh South (Glen of the Ivy) between Aghaglinny South and Cappanawalla hills (just over 1,000 feet high) I walked until I reached the gap where the bay stretched out beneath. The sun shone, the waters changed from deep to pale blue to green and purple, the wind drove the waves gently and all about harebells tossed in the grass as I sat and watched. I thought of the beautiful song of Amhairghin, the poet, seer and judge of the Gaels who came to Ireland in the pre-Christian era. Robert Graves translated it from the Gaelic, "…I am a wonder: among flowers … I am a spear: that rears for blood." The combination, if not union, of man's grace and ruthlessness echoes down the centuries from Amhairghin to Shakespeare when he has Hamlet make the great speech, "What a piece of work is man…". Amhairghin, like the Hindu Krishna and indeed Taliesin the Welsh Gael, seems to have been a symbol of creation's potential. As I looked at the light then dark clouds racing from the Southwest filling the blue sky, obliterating the sun I could believe the ancient words. Then the wind rose striking up white horses from a pewter sea, burnet rose bushes, hawthorn, hazel and holly trees swayed until with the strengthening wind they

September

Changing weather seen from the gap between Cappanawalla and Gleninagh mountain.

46

began to whip round and round. Land and sea, now restless, unsubdued, were as a mighty vortex, vegetation and water violently eddying in the sheeting rain. I hurried down having witnessed

"...the sea
  And heaven rolled as one and from the two"
hoping for
  "fresh transfigurings of freshest blue." (Wallace Stevens).

September 1999

Wordsworth tells us,
  "Though nothing can bring back the hour
    Of splendour in the grass, of glory in the flower."
Splendour and glory we had on this morning in the fall of the year as we walked along the Burren coast by Cloch Bharr an Choinín (stony headland of the rabbit), Poll Salach (choppy hollow), Ceann Capaill (horse headland). Above and inland lay Dúnán Mór with its promontory fort, Lysacht's cave and Cathair na Gréine (caher of the sun). And indeed we had the sun with such a gentle wind – perfect walking weather. We luxuriated in the sounds of the old Gaelic placenames and in the profusion of flowers and plants everywhere. Yet again we wondered at the sheer variety of the terrain: broken limestone rocks, great flat clints with plant-filled crevices, soft, short grassland and high meadows all between cliffs of limestone, shale and rocky mountain. The scent of wet seaweed alternated with that of flowers and grass. And what flowers! We counted well over twenty different white flowers, the rest of differing shades of blue, purple and mauve: harebells, field scabious, limestone bugle, clover, marjoram, self heal, eyebright, sea mayweed, bloody cranesbill. Near some squinancywort we found rock samphire, in the grykes hemp agrimony, blackthorn (no sloes) and wall rue. The miniature suns of carline thistles in clusters everywhere. Little clumps of Irish saxifrage lingered, the fat black hips of burnet roses shone and downy remains of mountain avens were tawny in the sunshine. All this plenitude is of the Burren, of its limestone core, its very heart. However

Cathair na Gréine – *Caher of the Sun.*

on this calcareous stone, on its wide pavements, ling or Irish heather also flourished and flourishes. Yet another Burren marvel because, of course, as we know, like all heathers it favours only peaty soil which it has found in bowls and hollows on top of the limestone. Strange, beautiful land and what a glorious walk of watching the ocean's slightly ruffled blue surface, its roar muted, quietness reigning. In the distance Inis Oírr, Inis Meáin, Inis Mór – the Aran Islands. Back in August one sunny morning my feet became very cold, the light changed becoming similar to the evening light when everything is so distinct, each hanging fuchsia bell eminently single, each woodbine (honeysuckle) whorl individual. No bird flew – no bird was visible. It was the eclipse of the sun, its
  "excess/Of glory obscur'd" (Milton). Ah well!
  "Clouds and eclipses stain both moon and sun."
  (Shakespeare).

October 1988

Early this morning from our window, through our field glasses, we saw on the Rine, that claw of land that stretches out into our bay, four cormorants standing in line on the sand. One by one they stretched out their wings, remaining immobile but almost as if they were to begin some ritual pagan dance. Later, on our walk to the village, we stop to look at the mud flats, to watch the oystercatchers and a curlew feed. One of our resident herons flies down to be chased away by the other which suddenly emerges from behind a rock. The great birds fill the sky. Even the curlew looks up but the oystercatchers are too busy to pay any attention. In the village harbour we are very pleased to see that our resident swans still police the one cygnet left to them. Last year our seals killed all. This year they got three out of four. We walk to the Rine and on it in the afternoon. The roadside hedges are still beautifully green with the wild fuchsia, flowering since early May this year, and the thick-berried hawthorn, the green touched with red and the sloes with the bloom of black grapes. Though we wouldn't like to burst one of them against "our palate fine"! In damp soil on the path to the Rine we notice a small hoof mark and to our great joy we see on the rocks and among their hollows our herd of wild goats, down from the hills. We had not seen them since last year. The herd has increased in numbers and there are kids. The purple heather, clusters of harebells and sea mayweed still linger and in the grykes here on our own property and further afield we discover the delicate maidenhair fern.

October 1991

I see two herons, each perched on a large rock above the ocean's surface and between them, on lower rocks, seals and cormorants, some of the latter with wings outstretched. Overhead eight geese in V-formation wing for the open sea. Later another six follow. Light spreads, strengthens into full morning; colours change – slashes of flame, pale lime turns to red; slowly clouds cluster, accumulate until the waters shift into soft grey and silver with the hills green and light mauve. Not all the dawns of the past summer have been so fine or indeed visible. I remember once writing that even on wet days there is a clearing when a walk is possible. This summer proved me wrong and well I remember standing looking out at the bay and thinking if I were a stranger I would not even know it was there so impenetrable was the draping mist, so omnipresent the sheeting rain. How glad I was then of our paintings by the Cornish artist, Mary Martin and the Irish artist, Manus Walsh. I could see again the loveliness of the Tamar Valley – sunlit grasses, bluebells in Cotehele Woods, hill villages in Provence created by Mary. Invisible outside, *Burren Moon Rising*, painted in spring by Manus delighted us, his Chilean paintings too. We look at a landscape and rejoice in it. Good artists like these, combining in their creative insight, integrity, truth and beauty, let us share their vision. We end by sight and imagination with several versions of the same landscape: our original view, the artist's embodiment of it and, coloured, framed by this the prospect observed again. So enriched we return to the paintings to have life re-enhanced, saying with Monet, "...to him who lived there, this room would have offered the refuge of a peaceable meditation." Rain sluices down. I am startled to see a bird, only the head visible, staring at me from the window-top. A wagtail, feet grasping the ledge-top, picking off snails, small, pink-shelled, whorls silver-edged. These will not "come and join the dance."

November 1987

Almost every autumn and winter day we walk. Some mornings, the hills completely obscured in mist, Galway Bay is practically invisible, sombre under sheeting rain. Yet often on the greyest of days there is a lightening over the sea. Winds disperse the clouds, light thins, gold threads the hills, green fields shimmer, the lovely valley lies fertile, the whole area renewing itself in very visible beauty, and out we go. The air in winter has a delicate crispness. In November, in a sheltered patch of our land, we have primroses in bloom. In winter months the cattle,

Burren Moon Rising.

sheep and wild goats go up the hills to graze, unlike Switzerland. In this landscape, bare for the most part of trees, the colours are still those of autumn and winter. The bracken, heather, hazel groves, rowan and hawthorn trees produce all shades of brown, gold and red. Sometimes branches of glowing wild fuchsia linger in the hedges. Holly trees are polished green often weighted with crimson berries. It is a landscape of austerity, stripped to limestone pavements cut through by fissures. It strikes a certain purity of spirit. The fertile areas save it from both gloom and poverty. This is the season for the turloughs – disappearing loughs. They fill and drain away into rivers that run mostly underground. The choughs still seem to come to their old nest. The same pair breed each year in the O'Loghlen tower at Gleninagh by the sea. Blue tits winter in the hazel groves. Chaffinches, blackbirds and, of course, magpies and jackdaws come for the crumbs. Yesterday a fox leapt our stone wall. On Loch Muirí we counted 61 swans, all of them children of Lir, the sea god.

November 1988

A storm of wind and rain hit us so we immediately drove to Doolin harbour to watch the beating ocean from the safety of the car. In such tempests it is much too dangerous to walk close to the sea. People have been struck by giant waves on this coast, swept away and drowned in minutes. Local people pass on their respect for this stupendous force. Meanwhile the sight of the high, spuming waves, their cold green as they speed ever stretching upward before their break, crash and thunder against pier and rocks is, as my brother believes, hypnotic. He would also echo O'Neill, "Dat ole davil sea". Dense waves of mist obliterate the Aran Islands; the nearest about forty minutes' boat trip from here. No boats will crest these mountains of waves. Not a living creature is visible, not even "The bird, the beating bird, extending wings" (Shakespeare) could survive this maelstrom. It is at once exciting, passionate and humbling. We return home to shelter and warmth to find everything washed clean, glittering green and sharp, a water underworld. Later,

when the turmoil is over, a huge grey/black cloud moves low over the sparkling valley while all around it the sun emits a saffron light. Into this glide four common terns, their wings white when wheeling near the cloud but touched with gold when sheering into the saffron. Soon they begin to fly "with swallows' wings," dipping, rising, turning, falling, "The common sun, the air, the skies" to them "are opening paradise". (Thomas Gray). More and more terns arrive, all of them swooping, diving for the insects that rise from the warm, wet earth. For a moment they make us "meaner creatures kings". (Shakespeare).

November 1989

After three weeks of almost unremitting rain, storm and wind we are shaking ourselves like drenched dogs. It was impossible to walk by the sea for fear of being swept in. Outside the shelter of Galway Bay the waves ripped and roared against everything in their way. Spumes of salt cut our faces, crusting them white. The wind, full-bellied, dumped slanting avalanches of rain on rock, clint, gryke, field and garden. Turloughs filled to the rim, overflowed and covered the roads. Short power-cuts of two to twenty minutes struck us. Car engines sputtered and died, ours on a flooded road. We were pushed out by two young girls, all of us laughing. What more can we do, when as Mills, that wonderful American naturalist, would have it, "Irresistible is nature's call to play"? Today the wind is quiet and we walked the Newtown Castle back lane, rutted, with grass in the middle – a lovely sight in days of tarmacadam, with reminders of what the same lane was like before our three-week old storm. Holly glistens in the sun, its berries changing colour from tree to tree, deep red to orange. The wild fuchsia has dropped its flowers except in the very centre of the sheltered bushes. Hazel trees hold their catkins but the nuts have fallen. What we think is calli carpi, its oval ochre leaves veined with rose, droop their sprays of pendant dark pink berries like crushed strawberries mixed with cream! I am reminded of all the marvellous *Guardian* readers who wrote

Green road at Gleninagh.

November 1990

Across Ballyvaughan Bay at dawn a drop curtain of almost navy cloud extended, lifting gradually to let in the light, pale at first, then burnished, living. Darkness on the ocean dispersed. Its whole surface began to shimmer, to shift unceasingly in rucks of small waves. The hills and martello tower on Finavarra became visible – the backdrop. The diurnal drama commenced. A curlew flew overhead soon followed by a woodcock. A chaffinch sidled up to another on the wires, from time to time glancing at each other until a third chaffinch landed to chase the sidler away. On 6th November, we walked almost the length of the valley towards Feenagh. In several places, sheltered in crevices of limestone slabs, we saw bloody cranesbill, a few harebells and some field scabious. Rathborney River, a stream really, beautifully clear, rushed by swollen with all the rains of October. In ruined Rathborney church there is a gleaming white plaque set high in the wall, commemorating a captain from North Carolina in the United States Medical Corps 1914-1918. At home we found, way at the back of our three acres of Burren, one perfect burnet rose and saw the brown, dark-red streak of a stoat flash by. On 7th November, again in brilliant sun, above the deepest of blue seas we walked the Old Road, grass-covered, high in Gleninagh Mountain, from Murrough near Fanore, to beyond Black Head. Here the lichens were abundant, white, pale green and bright orange on the Burren drystone walls. The hawthorn trees, growing low because of the wind, were almost encrusted with a light green shading to white lichen, among which the dark berries gleamed. At night the moon lies full upon the high tide, making a silver highway across the village bay. And so we

"...pluck till time and times are done
The silver apples of the moon,
The golden apples of the sun." (Yeats).

so beautifully to me and I thank the Fates for them and for the beauty of storm and calm. Moss and ferns so drought-stricken in the dry summer are verdant. Our hills are shades of muted brown, so different from New England's glory. The brilliant green of our Ballyvaughan valley under blue skies and beside an azure sea is an "agate cup of jade". (Yeats).

November 1991

The air is still; no wind moves among the low bushes. No sound surfaces. Autumn sun gilds Loch Gealáin, transforming from brown to titian the bracken of the further hills. Before us lies the six hundred feet of Mullaghmore (translation – great summit). There are higher hills in the Burren but there are none more dramatic. Wind, rain, sun and the cold of frost through aeons have sculpted the terraced limestone in a surging upward sweep that inspires wonder, peace and gentle thoughts. As we walk, this late in the year, we discover the remains of summer, early autumn, and even spring. At the foot of Mullaghmore we find swathes of shrubby cinquefoil (*Potentilla fruticosa*) with a few lingering yellow flowers. In drier areas the startling deep pink petals of some bloody cranesbill (*Geranium sanguineum*) attract us. On the lowest slopes the dark green of mountain avens (*Dryas octopetala*) covers the limestone. As we wander we come upon grass-of-Parnassus (*Parnassia palustris*); the white flowers pure as the driven snow, the heart-shaped leaves green and glistening. And here, in this most secluded and lovely place, the imagination takes off and,

Grass of Parnassus.

since we have just returned from Mount Parnassus, Greece, home of the god Apollo, the flight has a classical surge – apologies to classicists! Apollo was, according to legend, reared away from Greece, either in Lycia or the land of the Hyperboreans (taken to be these Western Islands). Indeed each autumn, leaving his temple at Delphi beneath Mount Parnassus, he returns to this land. I think Mullaghmore is his home for nearly half the year! All that is beneficent, light-giving and harmonious in the god he would find mirrored in this earthly quietness, remoteness, this treasure-laden region of Mullaghmore. Here, what relief he would experience, to escape the ceaseless coach lines of his Grecian home. His relief may be short-lived, dependent on an environmental impact study on the advisability of siting, just over a mile from Mullaghmore, an interpretive centre with coach and car parks. We may no longer be able to say with Keats,

"Round many western islands have I been
  Which bards in fealty to Apollo hold."

November 1998

Poor Nellie is dead. Jo and Sheila Burns' donkey aged approximately thirty-five. I wrote some years ago about Nellie's nocturnal habit (2-3 am!) of braying for her few slices of bread and Jo staggering out to give them. We miss Nellie now when we walk that arm of land, the Rine, which juts out into the bay. Although it is opposite our house we have a fifteen-minute walk by road to reach its beginning. We tried at low tide to walk across from our house but I fell in and my boots filled with mud! So life on the Rine has changed. I am assured that there's to be a new donkey foal to join the grazing cattle. This, however, is not the only change on the Rine. Almost two decades ago it had level dunes, grassed and flower-strewn, with its limestone pavements walkable at the ebb and between it and the coast a small mudflat for waders. Over the years the mighty Atlantic waves have breached the dunes in places flinging boulders, rocks and stones in the gaps. Now in 1998 there are further breaches, some dunes falling away to make half-moons of golden sand. Small crescent beaches edged always by the great limestone clints where swaying in tidal motion are cord-like seaweed, (*Chorda filum*), delicate white carrigeen (*Chondrus crispus*) together with huge bunches of brown bladderweed whose reproductive receptacles release into low tides for union thousands of eggs and sperm. Such enormous numbers being indicative of the difficulty of fertilisation and survival in the aquatic environment. Between the Rine and the coast the sandy mudflat, the feeding ground for waders, has increased three-fold. As Spenser writes,

"...The ever-whirling wheel
Of change; the which all mortal things doth sway".

November 1999

Two hooded crows (carrion crows) perched on a branch, watched, as I did standing by the harbour wall, the drama in Ballyvaughan Bay. A herring gull was annoying one of our resident herons. It kept darting in close and flying away again. The heron stabbed at it with its stiletto beak. This did not stop the gull. At last with a great harsh cry the heron spread its wings, rose mightily into the air to chase the gull. They flew past the hooded crows, out of my sight, but the crows turned their heads to watch. Then the two antagonists returned, this time the heron chased by the gull. I thought to myself, being a foolish human creature, "This could go on all day." It did not,

of course, birds having plenty of common sense. It ended with the heron back on its original seaweed covered rock, the gull alighting on a rock opposite, with one of our swans feeding on the sea between them. The hooded crows flew away. I then drove to Lough Muiri beside the Flaggy Shore to see the whooper swans, alerted to their arrival by another annual and autumnal visitor – Dr Kingdom from Devon. I was lucky. It was raining but a break occurred and I walked to the lough side. To my left near the sea were about twenty whoopers, six being cygnets, and to my right were about fifteen mute swans. I watched with delight as they upended to feed. For the first time I noticed how, when upended, they kept their balance by paddling lightly with their webbed feet. Clouds unfolded. The sun shone. Rain fell in golden drops. I could see the far shore distinctly. On the gently lapping water were about sixty black and brown ducks – common scoters. The whooper young came close to where I stood so I noticed their creamy pink beaks while in the intense light their pale grey plumage turned silver. I left, grateful for this "pure stretch of joy". (Roethke).

A Clare man, wet-suited, swimming underwater in Kilkee Bay, south of Ballyvaughan, felt bites on his arm and hand. He thought he was being attacked by a fish or lobster. The claw bit into his middle finger. He surfaced, wrenched his hand out of the water and attached to it was a cormorant. The young man described his experience as being "mugged by a cormorant"!

Boulders and sand dunes on the Rine.

Thoor Ballylee.

December 1988

On a crisp and beautiful day we take, from Ballyvaughan, the back roads for the forty-minute drive through Gort to Thoor Ballylee, Yeats' Tower. The long, straight road stretches far ahead, bounded by grey stone walls, fencing off the limestone-studded fields of the Burren. The landscape is flat and treeless but the sunlight gleams on the grey to white stone pavements and rocks and on the fertile green between them. Ahead something runs across the road, leaping the high stone wall with ease. We hurry to investigate. It is a fox with a large brush, rich warm russet against the grey and green. On he pads to the next wall, leaping it with the same grace. We continue through Gort, once the market town of Lady Gregory and of Yeats himself. We leave the main road to Loughrea and wind our way uphill and then down into a small lush valley with a stream and a tower house. We wanted to see his tower in winter although it is closed. It rises square from the side of the stream, which can be seen from every window. Trees and saplings grow everywhere. Soon in spring and summer it will be a paradise of green. We lean on the stone bridge beside the tower and watch the resident grey wagtails, with blue sheen and bright yellow plumage, flitting over the water, perching on dry stones, flicking their tails until they dart off again. Here, for twelve summers Yeats and his wife lived, rearing their children by the green fields and hedgerows and by the tumbling stream, like the wagtails of their day. Yeats said: "To leave here is to leave beauty behind." We are lucky because we leave it to return to a different kind of beauty, sea and valley and hill beauty – our Burren.

December 1990

As busy as the Champs Elysée, Piccadilly or Times Square were our field, hawthorns and holly, except that here the traffic moved and at such speed that it was with great difficulty I at last obtained identification. Great flocks of redwings and linnets flew everywhere, alighting now on a hawthorn, now on a holly and sometimes on the grass. It amazed me indeed that there was no collision, especially as the flight patterns were so dissimilar, the linnets dancing their way through the air while the redwings jet-propelled themselves across the sky. A redwing settled on our front stone wall with the clear bay and Finavarra's violet hill as a backdrop so that with the aid of binoculars I was able to see the distinctive cream stripe over the eye and the red flashing under the wing. We were "Brightened with joy". (Wordsworth). Later we saw in the distance, what looked like a guillemot. It reminded us of an incident some years ago and a good story (true) for a December evening. Our neighbour, farmer Mick Carrucan, opened his front door to see a guillemot. He stood aside and the guillemot proceeded down the hall and into the kitchen where it settled to the side of the fire. The host got a box for it and fed it on fish. A few days later the guillemot followed its host to the front door and outside. It then flew away. On investigating the bird's ring number it was discovered that it had been ringed in the Faroe Islands, had been attacked by another bird and so had emigrated!

A time for joy, not least in the December inauguration here of our young, highly intelligent, liberal-minded, environmentally conscious President. A wish fulfilment for all of us *Guardian* readers, so

"…with an eye made quiet by the power
Of harmony, and the deep power of joy
We see into the life of things." (Wordsworth).

December 1991

At the request of our visitor, Sandra Siegel, reared in urban America whose ancestors departed the Polish/Russian borders, we set out on a hill walk to discover a deserted village on a day of sweet, gentle wind and sunlight. So, with Cappanawalla mountain behind and Gleninagh mountain facing us, we climbed until we reached the tumbled stones of what might have been a chapel, Cathair an Áird Rois – (ring fort of the high wood), the trees long gone. We then struck across fields down towards the Caher River and the Khyber Pass (sic) – how

much our two nations have in common! On our way we met a young man, tall, slim and graceful – an ephebe! – striding up his own mountain. Soon we came upon Cathair Bheannach (ring fort of lofty peaks), our deserted village, set on Gleninagh's western flank facing Sliabh Eilbhe (Mountain of the Herds). Here we separated to examine the ruins of about six dwellings with outhouses for animals. It was impossible not to be struck by the skill needed to build these cyclopean homes. Large irregular stones laid one upon the other, tapering at the gables to hold the roofs. We walked the rough flagstones leading from house to house. Leading away from the deserted village of the lofty peaks we walked in the reluctant footsteps of the villagers who might, in Famine times, have escaped to loftier peaks, longer, wider rivers although none would ever be more loved, none more heart-held. As we know the strong sense of place may be both a saving and a deprivation.

Not all our days have been sunlit with light breezes. Never do we look out upon storm-lashed seas without remembering the wonderful combined rescue in our bay of sixty-six French fishermen by the Irish Air Corps and the RAF in April. It was

Guillemot in box.

Deserted village at Formoyle East.

good that their valour and expertise were recently recognised when the Shipwrecked Mariners' Society of London bestowed on both teams the Edward and Maisie Lewis Award. To paraphrase Akhmatova- they knew the event and they braved what they knew.

December 1992

On a windy afternoon of sun and blue sky with massed clouds in implacable advance north-westwards, casting shadows of darkness on sea and hills, a world of camouflage, we walked the coast rounding to Loch Muiri. The contrast could not have been greater. The surface was in rippling motion and on it, to our startled gaze, was a fleet of toy yachts, their white sails upright. A race in this secluded place? And then delight and mocking laughter at our foolish illusion – the toy yachts were sixty-one swans, most upended. As we watched them right themselves, "Bright with joy..." we realised that more than half were winter visitors – whooper swans. They glided, bills black and yellow, heads elegantly erect, contrasting with the graceful curved necks of their mute neighbours. I had this sighting confirmed by an earlier one by West Country *Guardian* reader, John Leonard. On another day of savage wind, cut by lashing rain, the whole land and seascape a shadow play in an infinitude of grey, the precursor of storm, we saw four fulmars slowly, smoothly pacing the air thermals and wind spirals along the cliff stretch of Aircín (creek), Poll na Doibe (hole of Daub) and Cloch an Oilc (stone of wickedness) beyond Black Head. Beneath their controlled flight a rock pipit was literally flung about, lucky to effect a forced landing. Light spokes appeared momentarily above the Aran Islands only to disappear again in grey obscurity. Our friends Maura and Maureen, on their evening walk along the coast road, saw, through the darkness, flashes of light from high on Cappanawalla. They reported. Our sergeant set out with helpers to climb the mountain. At last they reached a young, very cold English couple. They had got lost and used their camera flash equipment to attract attention. They might not have succeeded if our friends had not taken their walk or if they had dismissed what they saw as a product of imagination – a jack o'lantern. What a perfect blend of ingenuity and close observation, not to mention a happy rescue for those "acquainted with the night". (Frost).

Mute and whooper swans.

The appearing portal.

December 1997

Our house was wrapped in fog. A few feet away our rosemary, lavender, heather, veronica, cistus and wild fuchsia were invisible. Then, shortly after 11 am the sun broke through dispersing the clouds of soft grey fog. Colour returned reviving the gold, scarlet and pale orange of the hedgerows. The sea turned blue to match the sky. I thought – "This is the day I'll write my diary about the Flaggy Shore, Finavarra peninsula. I'll have a long walk there, checking out the swans on Loch Muirí." The distance from our house, across Ballyvaughan Bay to the Flaggy Shore is about two miles and at least four times that by road. Off I drove in brilliant sunlight on a calm, mild day. Reality hit me smack in the face when I arrived – I was penned in by the thickest fog I've ever experienced! I walked the road beside the sea but no sea was visible. All I could discern were the grass verges beside me and the road under my feet. The sea might not have been there except for the waves' susurration, the briny smell and the call of an oystercatcher. Smell and hearing were paramount, the sense of sight unstressed. On a stone wall I came upon two rooks loud-mouthing! The grass dripped with moisture, hanging in limp strands. I reached Loch Muirí. Lo and behold – the banked masses of fog divided, a great slipstream of light hit the loch surface revealing what was before unseeable – twenty-six brilliant white swans and six red-breasted mergansers. So, "Here a mist, and there a mist, Afterwards – Day." (Dickinson). Nearby on the seashore I saw oystercatchers, redshanks and dunlins racing back and forth and then a flight of ringed plover wheeling, rising and falling, the sun striking their pure white underparts. Two yellow oilskinned figures seemingly within handclasp range passed in a fishing boat. Light was everywhere "Brightened with joy". (Wordsworth).

December 1999

Today I walked towards Cappanawalla mountain under dazzling sun, a blue sky fretted with white and dove-grey clouds with two rainbows arching from our shore across the bay to the coast opposite in Connemara. The wind drove the waters, their waves white-capped, in loud slaps against the rocks. Seabirds flew low in short stretches. Robins, blue and great tits and finches sheltered in the hazel and ash copses. I was thinking that later I would sit at my desk to write my December diary, the last of 1999, the final one of the century, indeed of the millennium. I smiled, remembering that in different counting systems this is the year 5760 or the year 1420, the Jewish and Muslim years respectively, each grouping dating time according to the events it deemed important. Such differences yet we all inherit and inhabit an earth of spectacular beauty. And truly Cappanawalla shone in its beauty, its grey stone walls washed by previous rain, its flanking fields burnished. And then I noticed on its summit a cyclopean portal, doorless, incandescent, inviting entrance, leading where? How was this? Often I had been on the crest of Cappanawalla and I had never seen such storied remains. As I walked and gazed the 'vision' disappeared and became two stone walls caught in unusual angled light. Like Shakespeare's Prospero I had to say, "The cloud-capped towers, the gorgeous palaces ... shall dissolve" and "Leave not a rack behind." However there were plenty of racks (wispy clouds) which thickened into dark grey congeries of cloud until half the sky was black. Hastily I scrambled over a wall into a hazel, holly and ash grove there waiting for the inevitable downpour. Blackbirds squawked. In a few seconds sheets of rain swept sea and land. In the grove great drops beat like metal tears on silvered ash twigs. The racing waters turned cold green and "mutinous winds... 'twixt the green sea" and mighty vault "set roaring war". (Shakespeare). Tonight I again walked our coast road, the mile from Ballyvaughan village to our house. The sea crashed in the profound darkness and the wind bent trees and bushes to its will. The diamond lights of the Connemara coast opposite were invisible, extinguished. But close to our shore lay a ship at anchor, riding out the storm, its lights brilliant in the blackness, its crew safe.

"Praised be the fathomless universe
 For life and joy..." (Whitman).

January 1988

We walked from the road across the limestone pavements to Poulnabrone portal dolmen. Over four thousand years old, its capstone ten by seven feet, it stands on a hill, between sky and Burren rocks that with the light alter from pewter to pale grey, to glaring white. In its own colour change yet structural changelessness, in the effect on it of its surroundings, varying weather and, above all, in this region, of the light, the dolmen seems to be a symbol of all life. Recently excavated, twenty bodies, six of them children, ornamental beads and potsherds were found. The bodies were the best preserved of any

Poulnabrone portal tomb.

discovered in such sites in Ireland, said to be at least one thousand five hundred years' old but now being carbon-dated. We had the whole site to ourselves and must have been so still that a wren landed in a bar of sunshine on the great capstone and began preening itself. What a contrast! The sudden sense of its humour dispelled our solemn, even ponderous thoughts and after 'our' wren had flown away we also departed without writing a poem on the site's long-since dead and its present small life. For our long walk we made for the hills near Ballyvaughan, our village – Aillwee (yellow hillside) with its wonderful caves, then leaving the path to climb to the top of Moneen (rough pasture). From there we could see Galway Bay. We stood in thin sunlight, the air pure but holding in its promise of spring an edge of winter cold. Over the bay clouds and sunshine mantled the sea into a soft grey, shot with silver. Spokes of light radiated from the sun so that, as my Cornish friend Marie Martin, would say, "the sun is drawing up the waters."

January 1991

The whiteness stretched from hills to valley, to seashore, the great Burren rocks overlaid, as if with petals upon folded petals of snow, wind-scalloped. It was 8th December 1990. Thirty-six years ago, also on 8th December, the same scene would have met people's gaze, with but few changes in the landscape. It seems incredible that between these dates no snow stayed upon this earth. The recent fall, described as heavy in the local, weekly newspaper, was about half an inch and, to us, familiar with a foot to several feet of snow in upstate New York, it seemed derisory, especially as the Burren snow had disappeared by early afternoon. Anything but derisory, however, was the sun shafting on the early yellow gorse buds, on our only holly tree left scarlet-berried by a flock of redwings and enhancing the luminosity of the planed or wrinkled limestone. Neither was there anything ridiculous about the storm from 3 am to 11 pm on 5th January 1991, with 100 mph gusting winds. The day before every news

Storm over Ballyvaughan Bay.

bulletin gave us dire warnings. The electricity failed at 8.30 am, being restored thirty hours later. Apart from the awful ferocity perhaps the strangest thing was the quality of light, never reaching above twilight but within that the greyness intermittently thickening and thinning, palpable and seemingly tangible. I saw, in the grey vaporous 'light' a rook beaten straight down through the vast, whirling wind currents struggling to reach the ivied wall beside a holly tree. It did. The waves at high tide were tree-high, "…mounting to the welkin's cheek". (Shakespeare). The day after the storm our windows, encrusted with sea-salt, had to be hosed down. Two days afterwards (today) the gorse's yellow buds lie under brilliant sun, blue sky but cold winds whip white horses across the bay. Our robin, thrush, blackbirds, finches forage under the bushes, "the sun that morrow" has seen.

January 1996
To return to the Burren is to experience always joy, pure and undefiled. Joy in the region's timeless, austere beauty of hills, valley, sea and sky, the tidal ebb and flow. I write at this moment, 2.30 pm on the 1st January 1996. The temperature is +10 C°. The sky blue over a blue sea – a zephyr barely stirs the yellow-gold of montbretia leaves beneath glistening holly. Two days ago the temperature varied up and down from -4 C° to zero. Our hills, Cappanawalla, Aillwee, Abbey and Turlough were snow-covered; the valley fields crusted thick with white frost. Poor wild birds darted low over the roads. Great northern divers and cormorants rode a quiet sea while further north in Galway's docks gulls floated on great slabs of ice. Throughout this glacial spell the sun shone. Indeed it shone almost every autumnal day so that the seasonal lengthening of nocturnal

View from Hag's Head to Aillenasharragh.

darkness was less noticeable than in rainy weather when packed massed clouds obliterate its rays. Christmas Eve saw lighted candles in village windows, the traditional Christmas welcome for strangers. The best Christmas story is of Jack, Mary Ann's grandson, aged six. He was the innkeeper in his school's Nativity play. He told his mother, Annie, he didn't want the part because he didn't want to say, "No room at the inn". She persuaded him to carry on. At the performance Jack opened the door to Mary and Joseph's knocking, saying loudly, "No room at the inn but you can come in for a drink if you like!" The best tourist story of 1995 was told by the inimitable Jim Hyland. "Two visitors from abroad were told by their guide, 'Today we are going to visit the Burren country.' 'That's good,' responded one, 'he was always my favourite poet.'" As Rabbie himself says,

"This day Time winds th'exhausted chain,
  To run the twelvemonth's length again." (Burns).

February 1988

We walk the Great Wall of Thomond, its ancient regional name, or the Cliffs of Moher, beginning at Hag's Head, the rock time-sculpted into a seated woman. Legend relates that the hag, Mal, chased Cuchulainn. However she was drowned off Loop Head, her body washed up here. By taking this route almost the whole stretch of the cliffs can be seen, all five miles from Hag's Head to Aillenasharragh. There is also the never-failing surprise of walking across fields to come suddenly upon this grandeur, the land's last barricade against the storming sea. No doubt there are higher cliffs, but it is the wild barbarity of Moher's sheer drop of 650 feet, their extent, their Monet colours, grey, mauve, violet and pale pink, which distinguish them. It is not difficult to marvel at them as the eye follows the black shale down to ochre sandstone, down hundreds of feet of Moher flagstone to the unresting ocean. Moher flagstone, we're told, covers the floor of the Royal Mint. The flagstones are inscribed with fossilised whirls and whorls of marine worms and plant stems. Branaunmore is the place to

watch the seabird colonies: kittiwakes, razorbills, guillemots, puffins and fulmars. Puffins shoot out of their sand pockets, wings blading the air, in arcs of flight. To choose a fulmar and watch it, its great scapulars outspread, unbeating, as it glides, soars, floats on air currents, finally wheeling before striking out for the open sea, is almost to fly with this glorious bird.

February 1989

Moonshine and silken kine (cattle). A moonlit night on the way to bed I look out and screech, "The cows are in." Raincoats are thrown over night attire, sticks grasped and out we venture, neither of us knowing anything about rounding up cattle. The dusty march of the longhorns in Middle America flashes through my mind as I "utter sweet breath" at the great, lovely, cream-coloured Limousin cattle. "Sook-sook," I croon. My father had told me this cast a spell on cows. He was wrong. For all our aches and pains we leaped from Burren rock to Burren rock like our wild goats. No people passed by and just as well, as they would have thought it was a winter Walpurgis Night. Finally we rounded the majority into one place but from there they refused to budge. I ran for help. It was nearly eleven o'clock. Our neighbour Mikey came. With no sticks but just a few words quietly spoken the whole herd followed him out and down the road. I slumped exhausted into sleep. Next day everyone in the village knew, one non-farmer remarking, "I hear the limousines got into your place!" Inevitably that night became henceforth the night the limousines got in. All this led to our being regaled with moonlight tales of the old *poitín* (potcheen – illicit whiskey) days – no one drinks it now. There was a very unpopular process-server who found a certain house always bolted and barred when he called, never anyone at home. In those days the *poitín* was delivered in five-gallon casks, strapped to the back. One moonlight night it was expected at the always closed-up house. It arrived all right; the door was opened, the poor householder finding himself face-to-face with the disguised process-server. No wonder he was unpopular!

Snow on the Burren.

February 1993

Great excitement and a quick dash for a camera. Snow fell on the Burren covering hills, fields, stone wall tops and clints. What a rare sight and plenty of time to record it in a photograph because it lasted all of three hours while the poor birds sat "brooding in the snow"! White earth met grey skies, hazed by a hidden sun. The sea pewter flashed with shimmering cold green. Eyes were dazzled. The sheeted Burren rocks took on strange figures, some like small animals about to leap, others prone in a white daze, domed, Byzantine cubes, rectangular shapes with Gothic roofs soaring like praying hands grew from the landscape. As Emerson expressed it, "The frolic architecture of the snow." Soon all was dissolved, snow into water, figures and shapes to their accustomed soft and wrinkled grey. Winds, gales, salt bearing, followed and waves as high again as the cliffs against which they smashed themselves. We observed the dramatic spectacle from a very respectful distance – people have been swept to destruction by venturing too close to this *ruaille-buaille* (rule-ya/bule-ya – tumult). To quote Emerson, again from the same poem, *The Snowstorm*, we were, "Enclosed in a tumultuous privacy of storm." Later, in a short lull of a few hours we did manage to walk the Flaggy Shore. Here the sea wrack was flung, some from depths of 75 feet, in mounds and great piles, on the limestone pavement. Some hanging, caught, spiked on thorny hawthorn trees in fields across the road. The variety was astounding: the rich olive of *Alaria esculenta*, winged kelp which used to be eaten in Ireland served like string beans, thin, brown cords of *Chorda filum*, dead men's ropes or devil's shoelaces, ruffled flounces of *Laminaria saccharina* and reddish seaweed or seaweed oak with its delicate pink-red blades, lightly fringed with felt-like tissue. All of them resembling belts, sashes and garments seemingly designed for some underwater ballet. Now dishevelled and torn, their vice-like holdfasts (roots) powerless against wind-storm and sea-crash. Emily Brontë would say,

"No coward soul is mine
   No trembler in the world's storm-troubled sphere."

February 1994

There is nothing more effective than a minor accident, eliminating long walks on the Burren's rough tracks, to make us even more observant of life nearby, to encourage us to read up on 'close encounters'. So it has been with me since I sprained my ankle. In our garden bloom snowdrops, primroses, primulas, winter heather, winter jasmine and of course our once bovine-bitten camillia. Just across the road from us in a lull during our still stormy and wet weather I watched oyster-catchers, ringed plovers, hyperactive sanderlings, dunlins, our resident heron, further away shags and brent geese. What caught my attention, however, were the curlews, their long curved beaks almost immersed in the mud. I wondered about this and later found a reference to curlews' bills and with it, for me, another natural miracle- a slight contradiction in terms! It seems that the curlew's bill is possessed of an astounding quality – *rhynchokinesis*. The length of the word matches the stretch of the beak and, even in onomatopoeic terms, its curve! Rhynchokinesis means that the upper tip of the curlew's bill is flexible, with the ability to open independently of the rest of the beak while deep in the mud so trapping small creatures like worms and insects.

Other reading on research at the Institute of Advanced Studies, Dublin – Aoibheann Nic Dhonnchadha on Irish medicine in 1400AD. The texts are all in Irish with Latin texts like *Lilium Medicinae* beautifully translated. The texts were used by doctors throughout Ireland under the Celtic system. Doctors had a high social status and had to train in philosophy, astronomy and cosmology. There were medical schools in all four provinces, with medical families like the O'Connors in Leinster. Regular bathing in a moderately hot bath was recommended, preferably on an empty stomach and after exercise. Moderate lovemaking calmed anxiety, helped appetite, led to sleep, giving gladness to the soul. The immoderate kind brought on debility and premature old age. Family planning was dealt with albeit by a strange means; a woman's right to contraception being implied. Truly, "Nothing too much".

Curlew and beak with ragworm.

February 1995

We left Dublin by train under grey skies and rain, reaching Co. Kildare where a spark of sunlight struck the golden burnished flanks of the racehorses on the Curragh. After that the rain continued until near Athlone where we noticed scattered pockets of snow. Then, as we moved further west the pockets became great mantles of snow covering the bogs, the small fields and stone walls. Ah, we agreed, the nearer we get to the sea, the less likelihood there'll be snow. At Athenry, Co. Galway we collected our car. We then slithered the twenty-odd miles home. We were wrong. The snow eclipsed the Burren rocks and fields. Our Burren hills, Abbey, Turlough, Aillwee and Cappanawalla were snow-clad, patterned in grey-black and brilliant white. On them the sun glittered while beneath the sea flashed bright blue to shining green as it heaved in turmoil. So dazzling was the scene that we could not gaze for long. Later as I sat at my window, I recorded the following weather changes in the space of little more than an hour. Blue skies and sea, snow falling, a huge ellipse of black cloud overhead being whipped along by gale force winds. Disappearance of the sun with the sea turning to gun-metal grey, waves crashing against the rocks, snow changing to pelting rain, almost night-in-day. Grey sky and sea lightening to the palest blue and the lightest, most delicate mauve, waves still smashing, the rain turning to hail, the sun transforming night-in-day to brilliant daylight. Last of all the hail becoming falling slush. This was repeated throughout the hours of light. While we were away we missed, I am glad to say, a power cut of over twenty-four hours. I have noticed a certain local pride in the weather conditions, "We escaped, thank heaven. They often get very bad weather in Galway and Connemara." Fifteen to forty miles away. It may link in to pride of place – what a bond it can be – in moderation! It makes "sunshine in a shady place." (Spenser).

February 1996

A life or lives in the day of your diarist! I rose as usual at 6.40 am, checked the temperature outside. Still -2C. Breakfast at my desk reading and watching out for the lightening of the sky. Then at first brightening I move to the kitchen where I have a better view of the sunrise. The hills lie dark, an almost even rim to the extreme east, then falling, rising, falling and levelling towards Finavarra and the bay shore. Light inches up – a faint green turning to pale then golden yellow. Great streams of red flood the sky, fading to rose, slowly turning fainter until light fills the air, bringing the hills to life, making distinct each crisp and cream-flecked wave. Later I go out to check a drain, the grating of which I've noticed has been frequently disturbed. Today it is lying neatly beside the drain. Who or what is the displacer – our pine marten or fox? Our robin, blackbird, wrens, finches and thrushes are about. Indeed there are two other male blackbirds. They watch each other but are not aggressive enough for a flying chase. On our walk to the village we see three herons, 'our' swans, oyster-catchers, waders and twenty-two brent geese. Our friend Emily tells us about the arthritic dog, Spot, she has adopted who began to grumble and growl. Emily said to her, "If you don't like it here, off you go and find someplace better." Later Spot was missing and did not return to sleep. Next day Spot arrived but Emily also got a bill – "Hyland's Hotel: Bed and Breakfast – one dog." Spot had got into the hotel, climbed the stairs and slept outside a bedroom. A young English couple were

delighted to find the dog there, joining in the hullabaloo to carry poor arthritic Spot downstairs. The bill was, of course, a joke. So this day ends with the writing of this diary as the light fades and darkness reigns.

February 1999

Two surprises and two alarms as I walked under Cappanawalla mountain. I detected a movement in the holly and hazel trees by the stone wall. I craned my neck round the trees and there I was nose to nose with a large wild goat whose great branching horns merged into the colour of the tree-bark. There we stood each seemingly as amazed as the other. Each as still as primeval creatures, each sniffing, I the goaty smell and the animal my lavender soap! I withdrew, leaving him in possession and as I walked I was filled with that strange and beautiful wonder at an encounter with a different species – our fellow earthly inhabitants. My second surprise was not far away as I progressed up the lane. I rounded a bend and there before me on both sides was a whole herd of wild goats munching on holly leaves. They looked at me, stopped eating and then decided I was either harmless or beneath their interest. I passed down the middle of the lane with a guard of honour of wild goats. It was wondrous. I noticed again the magnificent horns, some with ends whorled like great shells, some quite straight, others horned crescents, the young with small tender-looking protuberances. This variety was also visible in the coats, some shaggy white and brown, others a fine dark sand, yet others chocolate brown. I walked on, turned a corner but on my return they were still there and so stayed until a dog barked. Then the leader leaped the stone wall leading up to the mountain followed by the herd. No stone fell. I had been on safari – "O, wonderful, wonderful, and most wonderful..." (Shakespeare). It was a world of green and gold, the sun shining on glistening holly, gilding the bare tree branches, emphasising our still flowering golden furze (gorse) blossoms – a walk "in the realms of gold." (Keats).

Wild goats.

Tír Eolas is a small independent publishing house based in Doorus near Kinvara, Co. Galway. Since its first publication in 1985, *Kinvara, a Rambler's Guide and Map*, the company has continued to produce high quality books, guides and maps that provide information on Irish history, landscape, culture and tradition.

Tír Eolas has published seven **Guides and Maps**, covering the Burren, South Galway, Kinvara, Medieval Galway and Loch Corrib. They give detailed information on the archaeological and historical sites, the birds, animals and flowers to be seen and the natural features found in the area covered by each map. They are the ideal aid to the discovery and exploration of the Burren and South Galway.

Books from Tír Eolas

The Book of the Burren, edited by Jeff O'Connell and Anne Korff, 1991. An introduction to the geology, natural history, archaeology and history of the Burren region.

ISBN	1-873821-00-X PB	£11.95
	1-873821-05-0 HB	£15.95

The Book of Aran, edited by John Waddell, Jeff O'Connell and Anne Korff, 1994. An introduction to the natural history, archaeology, history, folklore and literary heritage of the Aran Islands.

ISBN	1-873821-03-4 PB	£15.95
	1-873821-04-2 HB	£25.00

Kinvara, a Seaport Town on Galway Bay, written by Caoilte Breatnach and compiled by Anne Korff, 1997.
Social history and folklore seen through photographs.

ISBN	1-873821-07-7 PB	£8.99

Women of Ireland, by Kit and Cyril Ó Céirín, 1996.
A biographical dictionary of Irish women from earliest times to the present. It documents the rich and varied contributions women have made to the shaping of Irish history and culture.

ISBN	1-873821-06-9 PB	£9.95

The Shannon Floodlands, by Stephen Heery, 1993.
A natural history of the callows, the distinctive landscape seasonally flooded by the River Shannon.

ISBN	1-873821-02-6 PB	£9.95

Not a Word of a Lie, by Bridie Quinn-Conroy, 1993.
A portrait of growing up in a small community in the West of Ireland.

ISBN	1-873821-01-8 PB	£6.95

The Burren Code 2000

The people of the Burren welcome visitors to Ireland's most extraordinary landscape. The Burren may look rugged but it is a fragile place and is under threat from increased human activity.

The people who live in the Burren depend on the landscape for their livelihoods based on agriculture and tourism. The limestone pavement, flora and built heritage are the resources on which tourism in the Burren thrives. Respecting and conserving this resource will sustain the community's well being.

Support the Burren Code and help protect the limestone pavement, plants and built heritage of this irreplaceable 'fertile rock'.

The Limestone Landscape

Much of the limestone pavement is private property and is being farmed in the traditional way that maintains the nature of the limestone landscape. It is offensive to landowners to enter their property and to damage walls and pavement – this is their home and their privacy should be respected.

Some visitors to the Burren adopt the recent fad for building miniature cairns and dolmens, damaging the shattered limestone pavements and compromising the natural landscape. Local people including schoolchildren spend their spare time on the pavements undoing this damage.

Weathered limestone has been used in garden rockeries for some time and the Burren's limestone pavements are being exploited to supply the market. Never remove weathered limestone from the Burren and avoid buying souvenirs or products made of weathered limestone. It is illegal to remove stone from the pavement or boundary walls.

Limestone pavement is protected under the European Habitats and Species Directive (92/43/EEC).

Plants and Flowers

More than 700 different flowering plants and ferns have been recorded in the Burren. Thus, although the Burren represents only 1% of the land mass of Ireland, 75% of the Irish native species are contained in the area.

Help protect the wildflowers of the Burren. Never pick flowers or remove plants or tamper with their habitats.

Parking on the limestone pavement or grassland damages habitats.

It is prohibited to pick or uproot plants in national parks and nature reserves.

Monuments, Houses and Field Walls

The built heritage of the Burren has evolved over the past 5,000 years. Sites such as prehistoric tombs, monasteries and ringforts are well known, but traditional houses, field walls and ancient road systems are also vital to the unique character of the Burren.

The more important heritage sites are maintained by Dúchas – the Heritage Service as national monuments. Take care not to disturb any of these monuments and respect all of the built heritage.

It is illegal to deface, damage or remove any part of the built heritage.

The Burren Code has been produced by the Burren Tourism Joint Steering Committee, comprising representatives of Clare County Council, Dúchas – the Heritage Service and Shannon Development working in partnership with the tourism industry in the Burren and with the support and assistance of environmental interest groups. The aim is to raise the awareness of visitors to the Burren and to encourage them to act in a respectful and environmentally conscious fashion.

Reproduced by kind permission of the Burren Tourism and Environment Initiative.